THE EAGLE AND THE DRAGON

THE EAGLE AND THE DRAGON

A STORY OF STRENGTH AND REINVENTION

CHRIS DUFFIN

LIONCREST

PUBLISHING

THE EAGLE AND THE DRAGON

A Story of Strength and Reinvention

ISBN 978-1-5445-0194-9 *Hardcover*

978-1-5445-0192-5 *Paperback*

978-1-5445-0193-2 *Ebook*

978-1-5445-0195-6 *Audiobook*

This book is dedicated to my three beautiful children, Briley, Coralie, and Isla. As I watch you grow and reflect on how your childhoods differ from mine, it drives home an understanding of exactly how surreal some of my experiences have been. I work hard every day to make sure that you never need to experience the hardship I knew. At the same time, I wouldn't trade the life I have lived for anything in the world. It is a life that has taught me many valuable lessons and imbued me with wisdom that—through this book—I intend to pass on to as many other people as possible.

Briley, Coralie, Isla, I hope that one day you will read these words and know you are in control of your own destiny, shaping your world and your environment. My highest priority in this life is to be an example to you through my actions, my words, and my choices.

While there are many other people I would like to thank for their support on my journey, I will keep this list brief. I want to honor my three incredible sisters, Melissa, Janis, and Amy, and my dear wife Jacqueline. You have been the most supportive and impactful people in my entire life.

Melissa, Janis, and Amy, you've been by my side since we were children. Jacqueline, finding love, support, and a shared vision was something I never anticipated. It has had a tremendously positive ongoing impact. Without the four of you by my side, giving me strength and believing in me, I doubt I would have made it through the darkest days. I love each of you so deeply. Thank you for being who you are. Your love, loyalty, and friendship bring pure joy to my life. I will always have your back, the same way you've always had mine.

CONTENTS

INTRODUCTION

As Ganya and I made our way toward the edge of the ridge, dusk began to fall. As we approached our destination, the landscape opened up into a meadow with a large rock standing at its edge.

The meadow contrasted beautifully with the oak trees. It was summertime in northern California and the hills were golden. The grass, feeling the effects of months without rain, was brown, but the leaves of the oak trees were a glorious green.

Ganya and I scrambled up the twenty-foot rock and settled ourselves at the top. Ahead of us, the rock dropped away thirty or forty feet, giving us a tremendous view across the valley. From this vantage point, we lay on the rock and waited for the sun to set.

As the sun dropped below the horizon and night fell, we saw lights from faraway towns begin to flicker in the valley. Up in the mountains where we were, there were no lights, so the moon and the stars shone brightly above us. We felt miles from civilization of any kind.

Ganya and I lay back and stared at the night sky, chatting about the things in front of us; the moon, the stars, and distant galaxies. We wondered how far away they were and what they were like. What was going on in those other galaxies?

As we lay on the peak, our thoughts turned to the people in the nearest town. What was life like for them? We could see the lights, but we had no idea how it felt to live in a city. To our young eyes, this small town of about ten thousand people seemed as strange and exotic as the distant celestial bodies. Our days were full of running around the mountains, digging holes and making forts, chasing small animals, and enjoying the little piece of the world we called home.

The lights sparkled before us, promises of a world neither of us understood. We didn't know that the town was small by urban standards. To us, it was a gigantic city, an entirely different world.

Darkness set in, and Ganya and I knew it was time to

head back. We pulled out our shared flashlight, scrambled down from the rock, and made our way back to the homestead. There were no roads leading to the house, only backwoods trails and secret routes. We were only four or five, but we roamed freely around the mountains and knew them like the backs of our hands.

On our way home, we passed through another couple of meadows. One contained the rusted-out frame of an antique vehicle. Only the outer frame survived: the interior had rotted away years before. When it was light out, Ganya and I sometimes used it as a place to play. I never did find out how it came to lie abandoned in those fields.

Ganya and his parents had lived on the land in teepees for a couple of years, and they had begun to build a more permanent home. Over a basic framework, the outside of the house was sheeted with plywood. The inside was bare, nothing but wood and a few installations. It didn't have electricity or running water. The focal point was a large living room whose windows overlooked another large meadow, which sat below the house. My mother, my brother, Pat, my mom's boyfriend, and I had recently moved in with them, sharing their half-built home in the northern Californian mountains.

As we approached the house, we saw both our families

clustered around the main living room, illuminated by candlelight, talking late into the night.

We wandered in, worked our way upstairs, climbed into our sleeping bags, and listened from the edge of the stairwell as our parents discussed politics, religion, spirituality, and every other subject under the sun. We were an eager audience as they ranted, discoursed, and tried to figure out solutions to the world's problems.

As we listened, we also talked. What was going on in those other galaxies? What was going on in those towns we could see from our rock?

Ganya, my best childhood friend, and I playing on the side of Sue and Tom's Mountain outside Ukiah, California.

DRAWING STRENGTH FROM AN OUTSIDER'S PERSPECTIVE

I felt like an outsider for much of my childhood. Growing up in the mountains, disconnected from the lives most people live, I felt a mixture of emotions.

Sometimes I was lonely, knowing that I was so isolated from much of the world. On the rare occasions my family and I visited towns or caught glimpses of a television, I felt a sense of awe mingled with jealousy as I imagined the lives others lived, the opportunities they enjoyed, the excitement they felt.

I wondered what it would be like to live in a town. Could I be comfortable living like the people I saw on my brief visits to urban environments? Would I be able to fit in, or was their experience so far removed from my own that I would feel like an outsider? Would city dwellers accept me, or would they feel that I wasn't one of them? Would I always feel different?

I'm sure you've felt like an outsider. Whatever your history, we all know the feeling of being separate from others. We all know what it's like to believe that we don't belong, that we are excluded. I've yet to meet anyone who has never known the anxiety and uncertainty of feeling like an outsider.

Those emotions can have a major impact on our lives. They can strongly influence our performance and our success, which is why we need to develop skills to manage them, and to manage the thought patterns they can lead to.

It's all too easy to become so isolated that we begin to lose sight of our resources. Every obstacle we face looks overwhelmingly large, and we don't know where to turn for support. Without resources or people who we can lean on, we may feel that the troubles of the world are on our shoulders.

In this unproductive state, life may look like one challenge after another. Our problems appear insurmountable and our long-term goals—where we want to be in five, ten, or fifteen years—look unattainable. In this way, isolation can kill our motivation, shutting down our ability to tackle the challenges in our lives and move forward.

This book is my story. In it, you'll read about how I moved from that life of isolation and uncertainty to a successful career as an engineer, extraordinary accomplishments as a business executive, and the pinnacle of the powerlifting world. You'll learn how I founded Kabuki Strength, positioned the company as a leader and authority in the strength industry, and found a happy and fulfilled family life.

No doubt your story is different from my own, but I hope you will find inspiration and motivation in these pages. I have faced some extraordinary obstacles and, in the process, developed and defined my mindset. Whatever the obstacles in your life, I believe you can overcome them with the courage to reframe your views, stay disciplined, and use your challenges to develop the strength you need to win at life.

It's my hope that this book will *inspire* you. That by reading it, you will start to redefine what's possible for you and take on challenges you may not previously have believed you could take on. I want you to chase your dreams, yet to do so with iron discipline and unshakeable purpose, in a way that delivers meaningful results.

I have completely reframed my life on multiple occasions, and transcended some extraordinary and challenging circumstances based on my personal vision. If I can surmount all that I've surmounted, I have no doubt that you, too, can overcome whatever you think is holding you back, enact real change in your life, and live in alignment with your vision for yourself.

As you will see, this book is more than a typical memoir. Each chapter explores significant themes that I encourage you to reflect on. Use the themes as a jumping-off point for your own self-reflection and self-development, and put the lessons contained within the stories to use in your own life.

My life story includes a dizzying range of experiences. While I wouldn't wish the challenges I've faced on anyone else, I used those experiences to develop a set of life philosophies. These are philosophies I apply in both my personal and professional life, and with family, friends, and colleagues.

In writing this book, I've identified the key elements of

these philosophies and examined where, when, and how I learned them. A philosophy is woven into each one of the chapters of this book with the intention of guiding your reflection. It's my hope that the stories I have to tell, combined with the themes covered in each chapter, will spark recognition in you and help you to take ownership of the principles described.

Not every story in this book is told sequentially. Each one begins with a story from the relevant time period, with specific relevance to the theme of that chapter. Sometimes these stories represent my earliest memories of that time period. At other times, they're plucked from the middle of that particular era.

Likewise, the stories are often grouped around the prevailing theme of each chapter, as opposed to a simple chronological retelling of events. This is especially true of the early chapters. Like most people, my recollection of my childhood is imperfect, so the exact sequence of events in those early chapters is sometimes unclear in my mind. Each chapter concludes with a brief description of the transition, as I move from one place—and one theme—to another.

I'm incredibly passionate about inspiring people to make changes in their lives. While we are all influenced by our environments, it's too easy to use our circumstances as an excuse. I believe in using the obstacles in our lives to spur adaptation, to grow strength, and as a catalyst to chase the things in life that scare us.

All growth is built on adaptation. The only way we can grow, physically, mentally, emotionally, or even spiritually, is by adapting to change. When we adapt, we become stronger. This simple insight forms the bedrock of my business and my life's passion: teaching people how to live better through the development of strength.

While I'm interested in the development of strength in all its forms, my primary business focus is physical strength. I work with people who want to get out of pain, create strong physical bodies, and live more powerful lives.

There are many different types of strength, however. This book addresses the other aspects of strength that are sometimes overlooked. Mental strength. Emotional strength. Spiritual strength. Strength of will and strength of character are as important as physical strength, and this book aims to fill a gap in the way we talk about all three.

Stepping out of your comfort zone will develop your strength, no matter whether you achieve your desired outcome. You may fail, but you can still use the experience to become a stronger and better person.

THE EAGLE AND THE DRAGON

This book is divided into two parts: the eagle and the dragon. These two parts correspond to the two tattoos on my body.

Between them, my two tattoos cover almost my entire body. The first is two eagles, one spread across my back and one spread across my abdomen, both shackled to my ankle. The eagle represents the realization of potential. It tells us that the only thing that can hold us back from growing, flowering, and taking flight in this world is ourselves.

No set of circumstances can define who you are. No personal history can hold your future hostage. Whatever has happened to you, it is not *who you are*. Recognizing the distinction between what has happened to you and the vision you hold for your life will allow you to move forward and take flight. It will free you to become who you can be and share your gifts with the world.

My second tattoo is a dragon, the Ouroboros, which eats its own tail. This Ouroboros covers my entire upper body; my chest, shoulders, arms, and upper back.

At first glance, you may think this is strange, perhaps even gory or cruel. The true significance of the Ouroboros, however, is as a powerful symbol of reinvention. By consuming itself, the Ouroboros also renews itself. By destroying our beliefs about who we think we are, we open ourselves to reinvention. This is a continuous, never-ending process, represented by the circular depiction of the Ouroboros.

This is the theme of the second part of this book: purposeful reinvention. It is about choosing who we want to be and defining the life we want to live. It is about the ceaseless process of redefining our ambitions and the impact we have in the world.

These are the two threads running through this book. The story of how I transcended an extraordinary childhood and realized my true potential, and the deliberate self-reinvention I've engaged in during my adulthood.

WHY I WROTE THIS BOOK

When I share parts of my story and my life philosophies, I'm consistently amazed at the response. It has a substantial impact on the people who hear it.

People have taken the time to email me to tell me that they were on the verge of committing suicide but were inspired by my story to save their own lives. Others have told me that they have moved their lives in a positive direction, by taking a new job or starting their own business. People who have been unhappy but comfortable have shared with me how they have broken out of the life they thought they were supposed to live and began to discover how they *really* wanted to live.

These responses come from the relatively limited sharing I have done so far. This book is a way to tell my entire life story, and to bring that story to as many people as possible. It is a component of the legacy I want to leave in the world.

Nonetheless, I want to make it clear that this book is not a how-to guide. I can't tell you how to live your life, I can only offer inspiration and guidance. You will need to define for yourself exactly how to make use of the themes and approaches contained within these pages.

This has not been an easy book to write. It has been demanding and heart wrenching to revisit certain parts of my life. It's uncomfortable to share my experiences so vulnerably. Nonetheless, I am determined to leave the world a better place for my presence, and this book is part of that determination.

If I could make one request of you, my reader, it would be this: if you find value in this book, share it with those who could benefit from it. Whatever inspiration this book can bring you will be multiplied if you share it with others.

The more people we can reach with this message, the more good we can do in the world. Let's reach as many people as we can.

PART ONE

THE EAGLE

CHAPTER ONE

EMBRACING FEAR

1979–1983 (AGE THREE TO SIX), SUE AND TOM'S MOUNTAIN AND SURROUNDS

Snakes feel strange. Their skin is cold and smooth, almost silky. The sensation as the rattlesnake's taut body glided over me was chilling. The rattle at the end of its tail flicked back and forth a little, indicating its displeasure. Rattle. Rattle. Rattle.

I held the snake's head in my hands, with my thumb and index finger on either side of its neck. Its mouth was open because I was squeezing just behind the jaw, making sure that the snake couldn't move. As it coiled around my forearm, wrapping and unwrapping itself as it sought an escape from my grip, I could see directly down its throat.

Moments before picking the snake up, I had caught it. Then I reached down and picked it up. It was powerless to resist. Its only options were to lie limp in my hands or wrap its body around my arm. Looking into the snake's reptilian eyes sent a shiver of fear through my body. If I let go or lost control, I knew I'd be dead.

At the age of six, Pat decided it was time for me to learn how to handle them, in case I was ever cornered by one. I always carried a walking stick with two branches growing apart at one end, so that it formed a "y" shape, just as Pat directed me. When I saw a snake, my job was to capture it. If it was moving, this was relatively simple. I could approach it from behind and trap it under the stick.

If the snake was coiled, this tactic wouldn't work. Instead, I had to tease the snake a little, enticing it to strike. I needed a long stick—rattlesnakes can strike about twice as far as you might imagine. My job was to irritate the snake until it struck at the stick, while staying a safe distance away so it couldn't reach me. After it had struck and was uncoiled, I could capture it by pinning it to the ground with the stick, right behind the neck.

I never got bitten, but we had some close calls. When I was six, my first sister, Melissa, was a year old. On one occasion as we sat together in camp, my mom sat near a bush, feeding Melissa. Suddenly, Pat began waving frantically at my mom. When she asked him what was wrong, he signaled anxiously to her to be quiet.

We soon realized that there was a rattlesnake in the bush directly behind her, coiled and ready to strike. Pat was trying to signal to my mom not to move, while simultaneously managing not to startle it. When she realized what his gestures meant, she managed to move slowly away from danger, avoiding sudden movements.

Living in that environment, learning how to fend off and manage rattlesnakes was an essential skill. Pat and I, along with the rest of our family, were far out in the mountains and we didn't have a vehicle at the time. If I suffered a venomous bite, there was no chance of reaching an emergency room.

Young as I was, I knew it was important to learn how to protect myself. There was at least one rattlesnake den close to our camp, possibly more. I needed to know how to handle them. They hid in the bushes and if we came too close to them, flicked their tail in warning.

The rattlesnake dens also affected the way we designed our camp. Rattlesnakes don't climb, so we lashed beams into trees, creating a rudimentary tree house, with our beds hanging among the branches.

Me and my brother, three years younger than me, played in the field next to our camp. Right by the campground there was a small stream, narrow enough to jump over. Ferns grew along the banks of the stream, while dragonflies and alligator lizards swarmed around us. When we needed entertainment my brother and I used to catch dragonflies, tie playing cards to them, and release them to race against each other. The one that made it the furthest was the winner.

When we weren't racing dragonflies, we were usually out in the meadow chasing alligator lizards. They were hard to catch, because they could shed their tails when they sensed danger. Most of the time, we grabbed hold of them only for them to take off, leaving us holding their tails in our hands. Their tails regrew, so we knew we weren't causing them any long-term harm.

Rattlesnakes were a very different deal. Pat enjoyed catching them. He skinned the snakes and pinned their skins to a board to dry them out. He planned to sell them to people who wanted to make them into boots, belts, or knife sheath covers. Rattlesnakes in that area were particularly large, so we got some excellent specimens.

We also ate the flesh. Pat told us that rattlesnake was a prized delicacy at fine dining restaurants, and that we were lucky to eat it so regularly. When we killed the snakes, we had to make sure we cut the head off below the venom sacs; otherwise the snake's venom would taint the meat.

We only ate snakes we had caught out in the open, never those that had struck out at us after hiding in a bush. If a rattlesnake thinks it's about to die, it may bite its own tail, making its meat poisonous.

THEME: EMBRACING FEAR

Holding a rattlesnake in my hand was an intense experience. I looked into its eyes and all I saw was its desire to end my life. The snake wanted to bite, to kill, and to escape. It had no other aims.

Every impulse in my body told me to get as far away as possible, but I knew that the safest thing to do was to stay calm, control my fear, and take charge of my destiny. Any movement I made from fear would have only one outcome: losing control of the snake and giving it the opportunity to strike a deadly blow. The only way to stay alive was to remain calm, regulate my breathing, and take specific steps to ensure that I, not the snake, remained in control.

The stories in this chapter come from the earliest years of my life. While some of my recollections of that time are hazy, many continue to stand out vividly, even decades later. These experiences shaped who I am and still have an influence on the way I live my life today.

I've collected them together under the theme of **embracing fear**. Embracing fear isn't about being fearless. That leads to recklessness and complacency. It's about learning how to mitigate risk. I've faced death many times, and I suspect I will do so again. The potential for disaster always exists. We master it not by ignoring our fears, but by refusing to let them dictate the course of our lives. Instead of running, we must meet our fears head-on. We cannot allow fear to control our lives. *We* must control fear.

A CHILDHOOD IN THE MOUNTAINS

Ganya's parents, Sue and Tom, met my parents in the early 1970s in a place called The Flats in Santa Rosa. My parents happened to meet here, too. The Flats was an old army base that had been converted into low-income housing, and which was occupied by a collection of hippies and beatniks. My father lived in a barn, along with Sue, Tom, Pat, and my mother, Cindy. By the time I was born, my mother and father lived together in the barn.

Mom, Dad, and me in Santa Rosa outside The Flats, the low-income housing projects where we lived.

My father, whose name was Daniel, was a very intelligent man with a broad range of interests and passions. For example, he loved to travel and had spent three years exploring the world. One of those years was spent living in the monasteries of Tibet. He loved railroads and ham radio. He was a member of Mensa, the high-IQ society.

Like the rest of his family however, my father struggled with depression. His mother had committed suicide, as did her two brothers. I believe some members of his grandparents' generation did the same, although I'm uncertain of the details. According to my mother, he was never the same man after he returned from his year in the monasteries of Tibet. She put the transformation down to drug use, although I don't think she ever really understood what happened. My father's depression was fueled by alcoholism, and he battled against both until the day he died.

Pat, my stepfather, was equally brilliant, as was my mother. I believe all three of them—my father, my mother, and my stepfather—were geniuses. Pat, however, adopted an anti-intellectual stance. He laughed at my father's membership in Mensa, preferring to express himself through music, poetry, and art.

Where my father was deeply intellectual, my stepfather lived for the moment. No matter the circumstances in which he found himself, he always maintained a positive outlook. He was an incredibly gifted musician and singer. He played with a number of famous bands from the era. Sadly, he was addicted to heroin, which prevented him from reaching his full potential. Instead of becoming a rock star, he remained a bar singer. For all his genius, Pat was incredibly impractical and struggled to manage the most basic aspects of daily life.

If my father embodied passion and Pat spontaneity, my mother remains the strongest person I've ever known. An athlete and a scholar, she was selected to receive an award for her academic and athletic prowess from a class of 1,500. As a young woman, she was on the path toward graduating as a chemical engineer. This was until she decided that she didn't wish to participate in the society she saw around her and began to forge her own path. To some she looked like a dropout, but my mother was no slacker. She was an incredibly hard worker who simply refused to conform to the roles that society deemed acceptable. She always had a plan to improve her life and no one who knew her ever doubted her genius.

About a year after I was born, my mother dropped out of school and left my father. She came home one day to see him and me covered in something red, viscous, and sticky. Fortunately, the substance was ketchup, not blood. My father had had some kind of breakdown and sprayed his home, himself, and me with the condiment. Nonetheless, my mother decided it was time to move on. She picked me up and left.

For a short time she was married to someone else. That short-lived union led to the birth of my brother, Mark, before she left that relationship and moved to Sue and Tom's Mountain. She brought Pat with her, on the condition that he quit heroin. She was extremely against the use of hard drugs and wasn't prepared to tolerate his addiction.

My dad lived for a time in this trailer at the top of Sue and Tom's mountain, outside Ukiah, California.

From the age of three, I lived with Pat and my mother on the mountain, in the house Sue and Tom were gradually erecting. For a brief period, my father lived on the property as well. He had a small camper trailer which he brought up the mountain as far as the roads would allow. This still left him some distance from the house, which was situated beyond the end of the roads into the mountain. Sometimes I put on my boots and hiked out to see him.

Many nights, Sue and Tom sat around smoking weed by lantern light and engaged in philosophical discussion with Pat and my mom. They were all very smart, so there was usually something interesting for Ganya and me to listen to, whether the topic was politics, religion, or something else.

My mother dug a fire pit out of the side of the mountain and built an underground brick pizza oven. Tom dug a hole in the back garden, channeling a spring that flowed through the property into a muddy pond. During the summer, Ganya and I occasionally used it for playing and swimming. Its primary purpose, however, was to irrigate the weed my mother was learning to grow. Between them, the adults had purchased some plants and my mother took ownership of the operation. Although she enjoyed it, her intention was to learn the trade of commercial weed growing to fund her dream off-grid lifestyle.

The hills in the area were so steep that they were almost ravines. To reach our home was perhaps a quarter-mile hike straight up a hill so steep that it was difficult to walk. We carved stairs into the hillside to make the journey easier. Eventually, the adults hired a tractor to lay a road joining our house to the winding gravel track that led out of the mountains. Ganya and I were lucky to escape that day with our lives.

The plan was to start the road from the bottom of the meadow where Ganya and I liked to play. With the adults at work, we were free to roam wherever we wished. Despite the fact that the tractor was running, none of the adults thought to warn us that we could be in danger. As the tractor turned around and headed toward us, we were playing in the berm—the giant mound of dirt that would soon be smoothed into the surface of a road. From the driver's perspective, we were on the far side of the berm, so he didn't see us. My mom tells me that she suddenly noticed what was happening from across the meadow and began screaming frantically in an effort to get our attention. Meanwhile, the tractor was pushing the pile of dirt directly toward us, seconds from burying us alive. At the last moment, I looked up and saw what was happening. I grabbed Ganya's hand, yanked him off the berm, and we narrowly escaped.

Living up on Sue and Tom's Mountain, we had a lot of freedom and connection with nature. On the other hand, we were exposed to a lot of dangerous situations. We would go out into the forest and build forts, where we often encountered poison oak. Poison oak is a low-lying shrub that causes a painful rash on contact. If we stumbled into a patch of it, we would return from our adventures covered in blisters.

It was a wild existence, uninsulated from the dangers

of accidents, weather, poisonous plants, and dangerous animals. On one occasion, Pat was working with Tom in town when snow hit. With snow on the mountain, it was impossible to traverse. No one was getting on or off. The snow lasted for two weeks and my mother, me, Sue, and Ganya were trapped in the house on the mountain, while Tom and Pat were stuck in town. Every day my mother left the house to kick up the snow and find some wood to burn. She brought her haul into the house and let it sit for a day, while the previous day's wood fueled the fire. When the new wood was sufficiently dry, she added it to the fire and went out again in search of a fresh supply.

Another time, my mother pointed at the side of the mountain and told us about a mother and her two kids whose car had gone off the road and over the edge, killing all three of them. Similar incidents happened about once per year. At the time, the road was poorly maintained and very dangerous (I visited recently and discovered that it's now in much better shape).

LEAVING SUE AND TOM'S MOUNTAIN

For all her strength, my mother was highly adept at controlling men. She tended to choose men who would do what she said. Later, I found out that she was abused sexually at a young age, an experience that surely shaped her attitude both to society and her relationships.

In her relationship with Pat, she was very much the one who called the shots. It was at her insistence that we moved off Sue and Tom's Mountain, initially to another nearby peak. It was on this mountain that I learned to handle rattlesnakes. This peripatetic existence was part of a constant quest for the ideal grow site.

We now had a road up to the house, but we still had no electricity or running water. Another family lived near us, and once or twice a week we hiked up to their place to hang out while our parents drank beer and chatted. My brother and I never wore shoes as we hiked from our place to theirs along a gravel road, so our feet became incredibly tough.

This was also where we took our baths. Outside their house sat a gigantic cauldron, raised off the ground, perhaps eight feet across and two feet deep. We filled the cauldron with water from the spring and lit a fire underneath it. When the fire had burned all day and the water was hot, we jumped in and bathed. Our soap came from the aptly named soaproot, a plant that grew on the mountain. As the name suggests, the soaproot bulb is a naturally occurring cleanser. We dug it from the ground and used it to wash our bodies.

I don't remember much about the other family on the mountain, but I do remember playing with a kid about my age. Like all young children, we liked running around and often got ourselves into trouble. One of our favorite games was finding nests of bees, knocking them from the trees, and trying to escape before the bees emerged and attacked us. Sometimes we got away in time, other times we limped home covered in bee stings.

It was during this period that my mother became pregnant with my second sister, Janis. When the time came for her to give birth, we didn't have a vehicle so she hiked out to the main road and hitchhiked into town. Unfortunately, the first vehicle to pass by was a dump truck. For some reason, the driver of the truck didn't invite my mother into the cab. Instead, she climbed onto the bed of the truck, where she lay while she was driven into town and deposited at the hospital. She promptly climbed out the back of the truck, entered the hospital, and gave birth to my sister.

Many of the stories I remember or have been told from around this time seem funny in retrospect. For example, I did two typically childlike things, unaware of the consequences. The first came from watching a cartoon in which I saw the goodies throw nails onto the road to pop the tires of the baddies' car. In an effort to imitate what I saw, I threw nails across the driveway of our home.

With money tight, we went through periods of having a

vehicle and periods when we couldn't afford to maintain one. This was during a time when we *did* have a vehicle. When one of my parents drove the car over the nails, they burst all four of the car's tires. With no money to replace the tires, we couldn't fix the car. I had sabotaged our only form of transport. Until Pat and my mother figured out a way to purchase new tires, which took several weeks, we hiked on and off the mountain whenever we needed to go into town or come back.

Another story I laugh at today was when Pat and my mom gave me some new Tonka toys. For people in our financial situation, these toys were a big investment. As a child, I did not understand this. Pat and my mom weren't thrilled with me when I decided to play a game called "trash compactor," smashing my brand-new Tonka toys with a hammer. The consequence of this action was that I didn't receive any new toys the following year.

Both of these experiences were good lessons for me about the realities of my life. I came to understand that we didn't have enough money to replace things that got broken. Buying new toys—or new tires—was a big deal.

Some of the snapshots I remember from my childhood remind me how unusual my upbringing was. I used to go behind the grocery store and dig through the dumpsters in search of discarded food, such as wilted lettuce. I peeled off the outer layers to reach an edible center. Looking through dump sites for items other people had thrown away was part of my upbringing until high school—I even referred to it as "shopping." Nowadays, this thrifty approach to recycling could be considered fashionable, so perhaps we were ahead of the times. An afternoon at a dump site was a family outing for us, much as a trip to the mall was for most other families.

A few episodes from my early childhood, however, appear even more sinister today than they did at the time. One in particular stands out in my mind. Pat found a drinking buddy whose camp was about a mile from our place in the mountains. This drinking buddy had been living in the mountains for decades. His shelter was covered in tarpaulins and he had fully embraced the off-grid, mountain-man lifestyle. On many occasions, I went and hung out with Pat when he visited his buddy. We hiked over to his camp and I amused myself while the grown-ups spent the evening together, drinking and shooting the breeze.

One day, Pat headed out to see him, so I geared up to tag along as usual. This time however, Pat adamantly told me that I wasn't allowed to join. Pat's visits became less frequent afterward, and I was banned from going with him each time. I didn't understand what was happening, or why I was no longer permitted to take part in the visits.

A few weeks after I was told I couldn't go with Pat to his friend's camp anymore, my mother borrowed a car from the family whose dwelling we bathed at. She told us we were all going into nearby Potter Valley—her, Pat, my brother, and my two sisters. We drove around for a while and then stopped in a parking lot where we waited for several hours. Mark and I got bored and found some cherry trees adjacent to the lot. We entertained ourselves by climbing them, picking the fruit, and eating it. I have a picture of my family on that day. My brother is holding a cup full of cherries, while my mom holds Janis. We are all covered in dirt, like stereotypical mountain folk.

My brother and two sisters in the town of Potter Valley, while the murderer in our neighboring camp was being arrested.

At the end of the day, we piled back into the car and drove back into the mountains. When we got to our campsite, my parents told me that Pat's drinking buddy was gone and that we wouldn't see him again. When I asked why, they told me that the police had come and taken him away. Naturally, I pressed for further details and they explained that he had reputedly murdered someone twenty years earlier over twenty dollars. He tied the guy to a tree and beat him to death with a tire iron.

Later in life, I learned that he had disclosed this story to Pat during a drinking session. Pat didn't want to freak him out so he continued visiting regularly, but that was when I was barred from joining the party. Just as Pat handled rattlesnakes by keeping the danger close until it was time to strike, he reassured his former buddy that everything was normal, then called the police while we evacuated the scene.

A NEAR-DEATH EXPERIENCE

Our third home in the area of Sue and Tom's Mountain was up another nearby peak. I believe it was known as Mid Mountain. Our house on Mid Mountain was on top of a ridge. Once again, there was no running water or electricity. It was a one-story building with a high ceiling and a balcony that functioned like a second story which served as a bedroom. We reached the balcony by climbing a ladder. There was also a giant steel ball that hung from the ceiling and reached all the way down to a few feet above the ground floor. I think it was an old bomb, which had been turned into a fireplace.

Due to the lack of running water, we got our supply from a truck that filled the huge water tower on the property. At the time I didn't realize why we needed so much water. In hindsight, it's obvious that it was so Pat and my mother could grow weed. This was undoubtedly a big reason why they chose to live on Mid Mountain. One of the snapshots I recall from this period is sitting at the dining room table, trimming a gigantic pile of buds and prepping them for sale. It was the first time I began to understand what we were doing to earn a living.

The balcony was protected by nothing more than a small railing. My brother, Mark, and I slept up there. One time when I was six and he was three, it nearly cost him his life. He fell from that balcony, the height of a second story, and landed on his head. I vividly remember him hitting the ground headfirst, bouncing three times, and coming to rest. His heart stopped and he stopped breathing.

Unlike on Sue and Tom's Mountain, we did have a vehicle—an old Buick—while we were living on Mid Mountain. We rushed Mark to the hospital. At this point my memory becomes blurry. I don't remember whether he received CPR. Considering how long it took to get from the mountain into town, I can only surmise that he must have started breathing again before we reached the hospital, otherwise he would have died.

A LIFE LESS ORDINARY

Many of the stories I'm relating may sound bizarre or outlandish; in comparison with the childhoods of most people growing up in affluent areas, they are. To me however, these experiences were normal. As a child, I had nothing to compare them to. Killing rattlesnakes, dodging bees, and narrowly escaping being crushed to death were simply a part of life.

When we killed rattlesnakes, Pat pinned their skins to a board and left them to dry in the sun. He wanted to keep our local area as free of rattlesnakes as possible, for our own safety. He also thought he could make some money from selling the skins. We had two small dogs living with us; one day they attacked the board and destroyed the skins. My primary response to this was disappointment. I remember thinking that Pat had worked so hard to capture and skin so many snakes and that all that effort had gone to waste. It never occurred to me to think that it was weird to live by a little creek off a meadow, with rattlesnake skins nailed to a board outside.

It was while we lived on Mid Mountain and my parents were busy growing weed that I started going to kindergarten. It was not a pleasant experience. I was used to roaming freely around the mountains, living almost communally with kids from other families. As soon as I got to school, I felt strange and different. It was obvious that the other kids in my class didn't spend their free time knocking bees' nests out of trees or skinning rattlesnakes. Kindergarten was the first place where I confronted my experiences and began to see them as unusual.

LESSON: CONFRONTING FEARS

I learned to confront fear so young that I wasn't even aware it was happening. I never made a conscious choice to place myself in dangerous situations, they simply arose as part of my life. As an adult reading this book, you have that choice. You can determine the fears you want to tackle and decide how you want to address them.

What are the big fears in your life right now? Once you've identified them, go a step further and list the obstacles that are preventing you from moving forward. For example, are you frightened of jeopardizing your security, or a relationship, if you change your career?

Once you've pinpointed your own fears, you can put together a plan for dealing with them. Fear exists for a reason and simply ignoring or overriding it doesn't work. If I had simply ignored my fear of rattlesnakes, I wouldn't be alive to write this book. I'm still here today because I acknowledged that fear and learned how to manage it. The key thing to recognize is that through learning how to handle and kill rattlesnakes, I not only limited my exposure to fear, but I also made myself objectively safer.

How can you turn your fear to your advantage and use it to develop your skillset? You may not need to capture and kill rattlesnakes, but none of us are immune to fear. We may lose a job or a relationship and find ourselves in an insecure position. The question is not how we can avoid fear, but how we can mitigate it effectively. What process can you develop for engaging productively with fear? How can you use it to make yourself stronger? How can you turn your fear into a source of power?

Fear is a signal. It tells us that we have an opportunity to grow. When we encounter our fears, we have an opportunity to adapt, grow stronger, and improve in whatever realm we are currently developing. If we wish to grow, we need to spend time in the unknown. If we're not exploring the unknown, we're not growing, we're not adapting, and we're not getting stronger.

Becoming familiar with fear is a practice. To a degree, we all need to consciously choose to live in fear—to prepare ourselves for the times when big opportunities come our way. If we haven't built up our resilience to fear in small ways, it will be much harder to master our fears when big changes come around.

Find the things that scare you. Chase them. Own them. Control them.

HYAMPOM: THE NEXT ADVENTURE

We pulled into Trinity Valley in northern California. Trinity Valley is a stunning environment situated a little to the south of the Trinity Alps—a series of striking peaks which are almost impossible to traverse. The area is mostly wild, with few roads and plentiful lush green valleys. In the summer, the temperature rises to well above one hundred degrees. The rivers fed by the mountains, however, remain ice cold, creating a breathtaking contrast. Up in the mountains, old cart tracks from the gold rush years are still visible, making the area look like it's come straight out of the movies.

The small town of Hyampom is set between the north fork and the south fork of Trinity River. Did I say town? Hyampom is more of a small cluster of buildings. It consists of a school, a general store, and a community hall that serves as a meeting place and activity center. The general store also includes a bar and a post office. When we arrived, the entire vicinity had a population of fewer than one hundred people. Hyampom's history as a gold rush location might have led to it becoming a tourist attraction, but for the fact that it's so difficult to reach. Traversing the twenty miles to Hayfork, the nearest moderately sized settlement, takes a queasy hour along winding roads.

Without that remnant, Hyampom and its surroundings would have been uninhabited.

I didn't fully understand why we had left Mid Mountain, nor that Hyampom would be my home for the next couple of years. Although picking up and moving was a common experience for me, the trip to Hyampom was by far the longest journey I had known. It also represented another degree of isolation. On Sue and Tom's Mountain, I could see a town of five thousand people. In Hyampom, we were an hour's drive from Hayfork, which even today has a population smaller than 2,500. Nonetheless, I was already getting used to the nomadic existence that would form the blueprint of my childhood.

CHAPTER TWO

———————————

HANDLING UNCERTAINTY, PAIN, AND LONELINESS

1983–1985 (AGE SIX TO EIGHT), HYAMPOM, TRINITY WILDERNESS, CALIFORNIA

The whole of our lives was packed into the trunk of our old four-door Buick sedan. On our drive we passed a lake called Lake Whiskeytown, beside which an old mining town was once situated. When the town became obsolete, the river was dammed and the entire population moved away.

Further along, we drove through the county seat of Weaverville, which lives on today as a tourist attraction themed around gold mining and the Old West. An hour past Weaverville was Hayfork, another small mountain community. From Hayfork, Hyampom is only twenty-four miles away, but since the roads are so narrow and twisting, the journey takes more than an hour.

Once we arrived in Hyampom, we stopped by the general store and purchased a watermelon. It was the beginning of summer, with temperatures in northern California reaching higher than 110 degrees. We then drove down to the river and sat by our car on the stony ground near the river's banks. The ground was littered with gray stones, many of them worn smooth by the motion of the river. My brother and I dug around in search of flat stones we could skim across the surface of the water or, alternatively, hurl into the trees in an effort to knock pine cones to the ground. When we succeeded, we smashed the pine cones open and ate the seeds as an accompaniment to chunks of watermelon.

I didn't know why we had moved to Hyampom, nor what Pat and my mother planned to do while we were there, but I felt a sense of serenity in our beautiful natural surroundings. Following lunch, we set off down one of the smaller forks in the river's path where we located a campsite and set up our tents. We only had pup tents, which are usually used as auxiliary tents for storage or pets. It appeared that we didn't have a more permanent place to stay, nor any solid plans.

A couple of days after we set up our tents, the rain set in. It rained for two weeks straight. Each member of my family was stuck in their own individual pup tent; so small that there was barely enough room for a sleeping bag. Every so often, we ventured out into the pouring rain and dug trenches around our tents to divert the flow of water and ward off the risk of flooding. We had no place to dry our sleeping bags, so we were desperate to ensure that they didn't become swamped.

Pat got a little stir crazy and went out in the rain looking for something to do. He found a big post and started carving it into the shape of a human head. Pat never could sit still. He was dissatisfied unless he was making or doing something.

Eventually, the rain stopped. We packed up our makeshift camp and moved further into the woods, up old dirt roads that wound deep into the mountains. For a curious six-year-old, this was an interesting journey. By the side of the road lay evidence of the old mining communities that were dotted around the mountains in the late nineteenth and early twentieth centuries. We saw small tracks, much smaller than railroad tracks, that were used for transporting dirt out of the mining claims. Although no section of track was totally intact, large sections of these old gold mining lines lay alongside the road on raised platforms.

After we'd driven for a while, we parked the car and

pitched our tents in a picturesque spot beside a creek. The woods were dense, and the creek was fed by a small waterfall that created a pool suitable for bathing. The pool was home to an abundance of water spiders that skirted around the edges and intrigued my brother and me. We sat there watching them for hours at a time. We also liked to hike through the mountains, exploring the old, overgrown roads.

Meanwhile, Pat and my mom were scouting for territory to grow weed. They were investigating the creeks to decide which ones could be used as water sources for our growing operations. Trinity Valley is separated from Humboldt County—one of the most recognized weed-growing areas in the world—only by a mountain range. At the time however, I didn't know any better. I hiked, picked berries—checking which ones were edible—and enjoyed the sight of the flowering bushes that lined the former mining roads.

THEME: UNCERTAINTY, PAIN, AND LONELINESS

The stories in this chapter illustrate the dizzying variety of changes that took place in my life by the time I was eight years old. Sometimes it seems as though the only constant in my childhood was change. By this time in my life, I was becoming used to my family's repeated moves. Every year or two, I was ripped out of a familiar environment and transported somewhere new, leaving behind everything and everyone I knew, except my family. With these frequent moves came a necessity to make new friends and establish myself in a new place. The only constant was the mountains, the trees, and the wilderness.

Although I grew to expect these sudden transitions, I never became totally comfortable with them. It was disorienting to find myself plucked from one environment and shifted to another. At such a young age, these repeated upheavals were dizzying. I felt as though the circumstances of my life were out of my control. As soon as I settled in one place, became comfortable with my surroundings, and made friends, I was forced to adapt to somewhere new. This naturally led to a lot of **uncertainty, pain, and loneliness**, along with a struggle to belong. The wilderness, however, was a source of comfort. I loved to hike the mountains alone, immersing myself in the natural beauty of the northern Californian landscape.

SETTLING IN HYAMPOM

By the end of the summer, we had secured a place to live. There was an old logging village where two forks of the river came together. In the short period of time that the mill had been operational, the occupants of the community had built several small homes near it. Since then, the mill had closed, and the original tenants had left.

We moved into one of the homes near the former mill housing complex, which was populated by approximately ten other low-income families.

There was little work in the area and Pat began to cut firewood for local residents as a way to bring in some money. My brother and I tried to augment his efforts by picking blackberries. Below the housing complex, between the river and the house, was a giant patch of blackberry bushes riddled with tunnels and trails. The main trail, which led through the bushes to the river, was always kept open.

Mark and I used to venture down into the bushes with five-gallon buckets and collect as many blackberries as we could carry. My mom cooked the blackberries into pies and offered them for sale to residents of the complex and other local people. At other times, my brother and I wandered freely around the valley, exploring, and playing games. We often played in the tunnels under the blackberry bushes and spent long summer days running wild.

Housing projects in the remote mining town of Hyampom, which were built for mill employees, but later closed.

Another source of income came from mushrooms we foraged. In the early 1980s, most people were nervous about eating wild mushrooms, but my mom did extensive research on the subject. She figured out which types were safe to eat and how to differentiate between those and the ones that were dangerous. Some poisonous varieties looked extremely similar to edible varieties, so it was important to be 100 percent certain.

There was a lot more shade in the Trinity Wilderness

than there was on Sue and Tom's Mountain. Instead of oak trees, the area was thick with firs and Madrones. The Madrones grew to great heights, casting huge shadows that provided ideal mushroom-growing conditions. Pat wanted us well out of the way while he worked, to make sure that we didn't find ourselves in the path of a falling tree, so he gave us the task of collecting as many mushrooms as we could. While Mark and I foraged for mushrooms, Pat dropped trees and my mom rolled the rounds to the truck. We replaced the Buick and purchased a flatbed truck that we used for transporting firewood.

One of my favorite types of mushroom had a flavor and texture eerily similar to venison. It even seemed to bleed. When broken, it oozed a viscous red substance. In a time when food was hard to come by, it felt sustaining and nourishing. We loved these mushrooms and ate as many as we could find.

Unfortunately, there was another mushroom growing on the mountains that looked identical. They must have been part of the same family. There was only one crucial difference: the second variety was fatally poisonous. The only way I could distinguish between them was to look closely at the substance that leaked out. While the tasty, health-giving variety bled red, the "blood" of the deadly variety had a slight yellow tinge. We knew that we had to be exceptionally diligent in our testing, because if we made one wrong pick, we would be dead. One day, the local sheriff came to town. He warned us that we would wind up killing ourselves one day. Thankfully, we never chose incorrectly.

Living in the mountains was dangerous. Not far from the blackberry bushes was an old car junkyard, filled with piles of wrecked cars. We climbed inside, under, and around the cars, looking for spots where we could create forts and play. Sometimes we huddled under old car seats. Looking back, it was a dangerous activity. The stacks of cars were unstable and could easily have shifted, trapping us or worse.

Playing in the junkyard wasn't the only time we diced with danger. On one of our logging and foraging expeditions, Janis was lucky to escape with her life. There were no mushrooms in the area, so instead of foraging, my siblings and I were playing in the mountains. After each tree was felled, we kids had the job of scouring the area and hiding any evidence that we had chopped down a live tree—the piles of sticks, twigs, and leaves when a tree falls. Our responsibility was removing them.

Although we were some distance from the trees Pat was felling, the slope was large. Folks were only supposed to chop down dry wood and dead trees. Live trees, however, were worth much more money. The way they dried and hardened post-cutting offered a much better burn, which buyers were willing to pay a premium for. For this reason, Pat sometimes chopped down live Madrones in an effort to earn more money for the family.

Madrone is a hardwood. The rounds that Pat sliced the trunks into weighed upwards of one hundred pounds, sometimes as much as two hundred pounds. My brothers, sisters, and I were busily playing down the slope from the trees when, without warning, one of the Madrone rounds came loose and began rolling down the hill like a gigantic wheel, picking up speed as it went.

The round hurtled past us at a rapid lick, missing Janis by inches. She was about two years old at the time. If the round had hit her rolling at such speed, she would have died.

On another occasion, Pat was felling trees close to the truck and one didn't fall as planned, crashing down onto the truck's flatbed. Fortunately, it was a relatively small tree and the damage wasn't bad enough to render the truck unusable.

Summer in Hyampom was fun, but winter was brutal. Cutting firewood in the snow was a slow, taxing activity, and we ran low on both food and money. For most of the winter, we lived off a fifty-pound bag of rice and a fifty-pound bag of beans. The store owner was willing to offer us credit, so occasionally we got a few extras. Both Pat and my mother hated receiving charity, so they limited themselves to only using that option when it was essential. They preferred to work for what they had. For us kids, there was always a little meat on the table. Pat and my mom went without. I recall watching them diminish over the course of the winter. By its end, Pat was smaller than I had ever seen him.

A factor that contributed to their hunger was the loss of almost an entire bag of rice. One day, I was eating a bowl of rice when I noticed that some of the grains had black specks at the end. I told my mother, who at first thought it was nothing to worry about. "The rice is discolored," she told me. When we looked in the bag, however, we found that our sack of rice was infested with maggots. What I thought was a grain of rice was actually a boiled maggot. The black speck was the head. I'm not sure how long they'd been there. Maybe I noticed the maggots soon after they got into the bag. Maybe we'd been eating maggots for weeks. We threw the rest of the rice away and rations became even tighter.

Mill flats in Hyampom. We didn't have much furniture. Pat is working on hand building a table from logs he split down the center with his chain saw.

A SERIES OF STRANGE INCIDENTS

Hyampom was the scene of some strange and alarming episodes in my life. When we lived in the mill housing complex, I had a dog, whose name I've long since forgotten. He was a hyperactive mongrel dog, short haired and very clever. In the short time I had him, he figured out how to open the doors in our house. Several times on returning home, we found that he had opened the doors to our house and invited all the other dogs in the neighborhood to come and have a party.

Sadly, he kept escaping from our yard and killing chickens at a neighbor's house. We couldn't afford to replace the chickens or cover the cost of fence repairs, so after this happened a couple of times, Pat took me to one side and told me we had to kill the dog. "I'm sorry you're going to lose your dog," he told me, "but we can't control him, and we can't bear the cost." Pat took the dog out, shot him in the temple, and tossed him off a bridge into the river.

A couple of days later I opened the door to the house to find the dog standing there, whimpering, with a bullet hole in his head and a flap of skin sticking up over the wound. Although he was scared of us after Pat had shot him, he clearly didn't know where else to go. Pat had no option but to shoot him again—this time making sure he was dead—and dump him back into the river.

On another occasion, Mark and I were stalked by what we believe was a bear. We were camping next to a small creek that flowed across the road. The road was old and disused, so the creek had reclaimed the land for nature. My brother and I loved to explore the countryside and see the other creeks that had washed out part of the road along the way. From time to time, we set out on an adventure and walked into the wilderness. One time, we decided to follow the path of the road and see how far we could hike. We liked the idea of living so deep in the forest, even though we knew that it was inaccessible by vehicle. When we saw a waterfall pouring over a rock, we thought of it as a natural shower. We looked for clusters of rocks that would be good living spaces or kitchens.

One day we were out in the woods, miles from our camp, when we heard a noise. We made some noise back and waited a while, only to hear the noise again. We decided it was our cue to leave. At a fast pace, we started hiking back to camp. About a quarter of a mile down the trail, we slowed our pace and listened intently. Whatever had made the original noise was still following us. We quickened our steps and kept moving.

The creature, whatever it was, followed us until we were roughly half a mile from camp. Then it pulled away and left us alone. Discussing it later, my brother and I decided it was probably a black bear. There aren't a lot of large animals in the Trinity Wilderness, and we figured the most likely scenario was that the bear had cubs and wanted to protect them.

We decided not to tell my mom and Pat about the incident. They allowed us to go out into the woods and explore. We figured that if they knew we had been stalked, they might cut down on those freedoms.

Hyampom was also where my mother became pregnant with my third sister, Amy. She continued to drink alcohol and smoke weed throughout her pregnancy. While mom was very against hard drugs, one of her friends—the same man for whom Pat chopped down an old-growth fir and rescued his chain saw—gave her and Pat some weed during her pregnancy. Later, he disclosed that the weed was dusted with cocaine. Looking back, I wonder whether my mom's choices during pregnancy had an impact on my siblings. Each one is smaller than the last, with Amy coming in at a petite four feet, nine inches.

Although Pat had little respect for laws, he did have his own moral code. That code was tested when a Japanese hunter was visiting the area in search of a black bear. In comparison with the brown bear, or grizzly, the black bear is small. However, it was still considered a prize by the hunter. A friend of Pat's took the Japanese hunter out into the mountains and they cornered a black bear in a big, old-growth fir. They shot the bear in the hope that it would tumble dead onto the ground. Instead, it got stuck on a branch and they didn't know how to get it down. Pat had a reputation as a good tree feller, so they called him and asked him to cut down the tree and retrieve the bear's body.

Cutting down old-growth trees is highly illegal, so Pat declined. He didn't want to risk trouble and he didn't feel it was right. Although neither he nor my mom cared at all about society's rules, both of them lived by their own moral code. The hunter tried to shoot down the branch of the tree to no avail. His friend, the guide, responded by attempting to fell the tree himself. He fetched his chain saw and started cutting. Before long, the tree was dead and his chain saw was stuck in the trunk, completely immovable.

At this, Pat relented. For people living in the mountains, a chain saw is a huge asset and an essential way to earn a living. The tree was already dead, so Pat saw no reason not to intervene and save his friend's chain saw. He struck a bargain with him and the hunter: Pat would cut down the tree in exchange for the teeth and claws of the bear.

Pat brought the head and hands of the bear home and used the teeth and claws to make art. The head boiled in a pot in the backyard for days, while we occasionally pulled it out and checked whether we could remove the teeth. I still have a necklace with one of the teeth attached to it, and a raw ruby set into the tooth.

My mom smoked a lot of weed. It almost backfired on her one day, when she opened the door of our mill housing complex house to see two police officers standing outside.

They spotted her marijuana on the table and were preparing to arrest her. My mother was worried about being arrested, but she was even more concerned about the reputation of the police officers. There were rumors that women had been known to disappear in their custody.

Pat was at a house down the block, drinking beer with some friends. My mom turned to me and told me to run over and get him, and to ask him to bring as many people as possible so they could observe the actions of the police officers as they arrested her.

The officers were faced with a pretty large crowd. Perhaps irritated by the reception they received, they took her to the next county over instead of booking her in the town jail that was only an hour away from Hyampom. Pat looked after me and the rest of the children for a few days, until he could secure some transportation to bail my mom out of jail and bring her home.

Little did we know that we hadn't seen the last of one of the officers. When he came back into our lives later on, it was under even more sinister circumstances.

A FRIENDSHIP AND A TRAGEDY

While we lived in the mill house, I developed a number of friendships. It was common for me to go on playdates and stay over with friends. I was in first grade and I felt like a normal kid. One particular friend, whose name I've sadly forgotten, invited me over to his house a lot. He lived in a big house a few miles from Hyampom and their household was a warm, loving place. Naturally, I loved going there. Not only did I get to experience the kindness of his family, I had the chance to watch satellite TV. Coming from the home environment I was accustomed to, it was incredible.

I loved it so much that I started staying there for several days at a time. I would get out of school, go straight to my friend's house, and stay there until school the next day. It happened so much that my mother decided to draw a line. One day after staying with my friend for about a week, I got out of school and told my mom I was going to his house again. She was adamant that I would come home that night and that I would stay at home for several nights before I was allowed to stay with my friend again. She was concerned that when I stayed at my friend's so often, his parents were taking on a lot of responsibility for feeding me and looking after me. She wasn't comfortable with them doing that, so she made me stay home.

I was furious. I was a well-behaved kid, and this is one of the few times in my life I can remember throwing a fit. Despite my anger, my mom insisted that I get in the car and go home with her. Eventually, I did as she asked and spent the night at home, seething with rage. When I arrived at school the next morning, one of my teachers called my parents and me into the school, sat us down, and told us that a gas line had broken in my friend's house the previous night. The house caught on fire. The entire family was trapped inside and died in the fire.

I blamed myself. In my young mind, my incendiary anger had somehow played a role in causing the fire. According to my mother, I was so shocked that I barely spoke for a year following the tragedy. My mom tells me that, in my sadness and quietness that year, she saw the early signs of the depression that had plagued my father's side of the family for generations.

MOVING TO THE ALIEN HOUSE

During our second summer in Hyampom, we left the house in the mill housing complex and moved into an old, derelict place on the other side of the river. I assumed we could no longer afford the rent on the mill house. Also, by then we were spending most of our time up in the mountains and the new place was closer to the wilderness.

The house consisted of nothing more than a frame, with no doors or windows. It felt so spooky that my brother and I called it the Alien House. The Alien House became our base when we were in Hyampom. While the house by the mill had electricity and running water, the Alien House had no utilities at all. Every few days, my mom and I hiked down the road to a natural spring, filled our water jugs, and hauled them back home. The Alien House was also home to a number of bats. The first few nights we slept there, we heard flapping noises in the dark and felt air rushing by our faces. We fired up the lamps to find out what was happening and discovered the bats nesting in the roof.

Outside in front of the house was a big pile of trash, presumably left by previous occupants. Everything organic had long since decomposed, but pieces of bikes and old appliances remained, rusting in the sun. My brother and I used the garbage pile like a toy box. We sifted through it for objects that interested us, took them apart, and built new things out of them. That was how we entertained ourselves.

Living out in the Alien House, we were highly isolated. Our only connection to the outside world was a tiny, battery-powered television with a screen smaller than my child-sized hand. At a guess, I think the screen was about six inches wide. I vividly remember watching *Star Wars* on that minuscule screen and being captivated by the story.

A SHADOW CROSSES OUR LIVES

Although we lived in the Alien House, we spent most of our time in the mountains. Pat would chop wood and drive between the different weed-growing sites we had established. He and my mother came up with a simple strategy: they found sites where one of the many creeks that flowed through the mountains could easily be diverted to feed water through hoses and into irrigation channels. They kept individual sites small and planned their locations carefully to minimize the risk of detection.

With neighboring Humboldt County known as a weed-growing hot spot, the authorities did a lot of air surveillance in search of clandestine growth operations. Pat countered this by growing his plants extremely large, because if they were close to the size of trees it would be difficult to distinguish between weed and other foliage from above. The plan must have worked because we were never busted during this period.

In some ways we lived an idyllic life, at least in summer. Danger was never far away, however. Large commercial weed growers were very territorial, and anyone who stumbled unwittingly onto one of their plantations was at risk of being immediately shot. In addition to bears and huge rounds of wood, we lived with the knowledge that if we ventured too far off one of the hiking trails, we might bump into someone with a gun.

Our camp was positioned to offer us maximum visibility. There was only one gravel road leading into the area, and it rolled around the mountains for miles. Factoring in the twists and turns of this mountain road, which made progress slow, we could see anyone who approached long before they reached us.

One day, we were sitting together in camp when Pat alerted us to the presence of danger. We looked out across the mountain and saw a trail of several police cars, advancing slowly toward us. Instantly, Pat ran off to hide while my mother destroyed the small number of plants we were growing at a nearby site for personal use. I was left to watch my younger siblings.

When the police arrived, Pat and my mom were nowhere to be seen. The officers took me, my brother, and my sisters and put us in the back of their police cruiser with the intention of putting us in protective custody. My sisters and my brother sat in the back, while I was up front in the passenger seat.

The officer who had busted my mom a couple of years earlier was now a sheriff. He sat in the driver's seat, chatting amiably with me while I asked about the police technology in the vehicle. The only vehicles I knew were old, so a police car with a fancy new stereo and various other police technology was fascinating to see.

I look back on my response and it seems surreal. We were being taken forcibly from the only family we knew. My brother and sisters were wailing in anguish. Yet I was chatting civilly with one of the people who was taking us away. Even at the time, I remember questioning myself internally. I couldn't understand why I wasn't exhibiting a lot of emotion. On the outside, I was cool, calm, and collected. On the inside, I was trying to figure out what, if anything, I was really feeling.

The only charge they were able to book my mother on was poaching. Approximately once per week, we killed a white-tailed deer for food. They were our primary source of protein. That sounds like a lot, but the deer in those mountains were tiny. They didn't make many meals.

Pat melted into the forest and avoided arrest completely. My mother returned to camp and was taken into custody. Although the police never located any of our grow operations, they took me and my siblings on account of our living conditions and placed us in foster homes.

FORCED INTO FOSTER CARE

At first, Mark and I were placed in the same foster home, separate from all three of our sisters. Before long, however, Mark's father took him in. I was moved to live with a new family in Weaverville, one of the towns we had passed on the way to Hyampom. I spent approximately a year in foster care while I was in third grade. I didn't know how long I would be there, I only knew that the state wouldn't allow me to live with Pat and my mom.

Weaverville was a scenic little town. Entering the town felt like being transported back to a different time and place. Much of the architecture has a historical feel and, in the decades since I lived there, the town's economy has shifted to revolve primarily around tourism. According to the most recent census, it's home to 3,600 people, a number I imagine was even lower in the 1980s. Despite being a small community, to me it felt like a big place.

There was another child in the home where I lived, and occasionally we played together. My foster father was a Cub Scout leader; on Saturdays, he did what he could to get me involved in social activities centered on the scouts. For example, I remember building a soapbox derby car and competing against other local boys in a race. Most of the time, however, I was on my own. I spent a lot of time wandering around the open spaces of the town, observing the tracks of animals and attempting to work out which ones had passed through. I preferred to stay secluded, alone with my thoughts.

Mentally, living in Weaverville was a dark time for me. I had no friends and once again felt like an outsider, alienated from the happy, smiling kids in the classroom and the playground. The warm feeling of belonging I felt during first and second grade seemed to have vanished with the death of my friend, a feeling that was only exacerbated by my isolation from my family. One pinprick of light during this period was a tape my mom sent me—the soundtrack to *Top Gun*. I listened to the tape incessantly, because it represented some connection with my mother. Aside from this bright spot, the only communication I had with my parents was the occasional letter my mom sent me from jail. I walked around in a bubble of sadness.

My hairstyle was as eccentric as my circumstances were stifling. I shaved the sides of my head and grew a Mohawk, as if to emphasize how different I felt. My closest friend was a peapod vine I grew for a school competition. All the kids in my school were set a challenge to grow the largest possible peapod vine. I talked to my plant, watered it every day, and even played music to it. Over the weeks of the competition, most of the kids managed to grow their vines to the length of a few inches. I think the largest aside from my own was about six inches long. My peapod, however, grew explosively. It reached a height of around three or four feet. I was proud of that.

One of the finest examples of my mother's indomitable will occurred during this period. Sitting in jail and frustrated at being parted from her family, she began to reflect on what she had seen and heard about the cops who had brought her in. The more she thought about it, the more she felt that something about the way the case had been handled was disturbingly wrong.

Eventually, by piecing together her own experience and other shreds of evidence, she came to the conclusion that some aspects of child protective services in the county were a front for a pedophile ring. She began to believe that some of the local police officers were implicated, and that they were deliberately preying on people living in impoverished, remote communities who didn't have a lot of resources or connections. This might sound like a far-fetched story, but she was right. The group was taking children into foster care with the intention of selling them into a larger, nationwide pedophile ring.

Despite her straitened circumstances, my mother connected with a lawyer living in Los Angeles and convinced him that she was telling the truth. He agreed to take on the case *pro bono*. As the case progressed, the details slowly emerged and numerous police officers were prosecuted and thrown in jail, including the sheriff who had arrested my mother for possession of marijuana. Due to the investigation my mother started, the man who was acting as foster father to my three sisters was caught as he attempted to board a plane and flee the country. He was part of a national sex trafficking operation, into which he intended to sell my sisters.

At this point, my mom was still unable to demonstrate that she was a suitable parent, so she called her parents, my grandparents, and they stepped in. As soon as they understood the gravity of the situation, they drove from Idaho to California, collected my three sisters and myself, and took us with them to live in Idaho. Meanwhile, Pat and my mother threw themselves into creating a stable family situation so they could reclaim custody.

Grandma with my youngest sister, Amy, in the Weaverville, California courthouse after taking custody of her and the rest of us kids.

LESSON: FINDING MY CENTER IN A WORLD OUT OF CONTROL

The years I spent in Hyampom were especially chaotic,

even in the context of an unusually haphazard upbringing. My family moved there when I was six and we left when I was eight. For many of us, this is an age where sadness makes an appearance. We realize that not everything in life is wonderful. Perhaps we lose an elderly relative or a dog, or we see our parents fighting, and we come to understand that not every circumstance brings happiness. Living in Hyampom and later in foster care, I got a massive dose of those experiences.

The biggest wake-up call in this period was undoubtedly the death of my best friend and his family. What's the difference between staying at a friend's house for seven days and staying there for eight days? For me, it's my life. Call it a stroke of luck or a premonition on the part of my mother: I wouldn't be alive to write this book if I had stayed another night with my friend. At a tender, impressionable age, I got my first taste of survivor's guilt. Relieved as I was to escape death, I also felt confused. Why me? Why did I deserve to live when my friend and his family had died?

Exacerbating these troubling questions was my separation from the rest of my family. Not long after the death of my friend, I found myself in foster care. The only connection I had with the people I was closest to came via an occasional letter from my mother, who was stuck in jail.

It was at this point that I began to ask myself how I could

make sense of the events that had turned my young life upside down. I had barely escaped death, I was torn away from my family, and I found myself in strange, alienating circumstances.

Even at that age, I understood that while we may not always have control of our surroundings, we can always control ourselves. In some situations, that may be *all* we have control of. No matter what life throws at us, we can always strive to master ourselves.

In foster care, I found solace in a connection to the wilderness. The town where I lived was small—only around three thousand people—but to me it seemed vast because I was used to roaming freely in the empty wilderness. Even in this disorienting environment, I found pockets of nature. I walked. I encouraged my pea vine to flower. I looked for ways to control my responses to the world around me.

My victories were small, but they were still victories. My pea vine thrived. I built a soapbox racer that was faster than the racers built by the other boys in my neighborhood. These milestones helped to pull me into a more positive mental space and kept me from wallowing in negativity.

No matter how much or how little you have, you always

own your reactions. Unexpected events will always occur. The sun will rise and the sun will set. The seasons will come and go. The moon will wax and wane. This is true no matter what you do. Ultimately, these events are part of life. What will you do when someone important to you dies? How will you manage your responses to the most painful and challenging circumstances? In the answers to these questions, we discover who we are.

Nonetheless, please don't imagine that you are powerless. You are far more powerful than you may realize. Even if you believe your circumstances are unalterable, look again. In my case, the government stripped me from my family. The central axis around which my life revolved was suddenly broken. For all I knew, I might never have seen my parents and siblings again.

In this deeply challenging time, my mother found a profound sense of conviction. The letters she sent me from jail reassured me that the fire within her burned deeply. In them, she let me know that she was 100 percent committed to getting out of jail and to win back custody of her children. It must have been so tempting for my mother to succumb to despair. Her circumstances looked dire. She had no place to live, no money for an attorney to fight her case, and few reliable family connections. Yet she never wavered in her determination—or if she did, she never allowed it to show.

Sometimes the best way to handle uncertainty, pain, and loneliness is to find small ways to attain a sense of control in your life. At other times, you may discover that you need to take a stand for what you want or what you believe is right, as my mother did. In the forthcoming chapters of this book, I'll share many more stories of both.

AN OASIS OF CALM IN A CHAOTIC CHILDHOOD

My grandparents' ten acres was nestled in a wooded area, with a creek flowing through the back of the property. My grandfather was a keen landscaper and he had used his tractor to dig out a large pond. He kept the lawn between the mobile home—where he and my grandmother lived—and the pond in beautiful, manicured condition. The property was dotted with apple trees and raspberry bushes and was fenced to keep out the hungry deer who would otherwise have paid us a visit. Unfettered by zoning restrictions, my grandfather had lovingly curated the land and dug a gigantic pond on the property.

With Pat in hiding and my mother unable to take custody of me and my sisters, my grandparents stepped in and gave us a place to live. At the time, however, I had very little information about what was happening. I was excited to leave foster care and see my sisters, but I didn't know where Pat or my mom were, and my grandparents didn't tell me or my sisters.

I think this was because they too were unsure what would happen, and they didn't want to raise our hopes. They didn't trust Pat at the best of times, and the ongoing legal uncertainty may have caused them to wonder whether they would need to step in and give my sisters and I a permanent home. Despite the confusion, living with my grandparents was a huge relief after the anguish and isolation of foster care.

RESTORATION

1985-1986 (AGE EIGHT TO NINE), SAND POINT, IDAHO

My grandparents owned ten acres of land near a small town called Sand Point, in the panhandle of Idaho, close to the Canadian border. The scenery was stunningly beautiful—that part of Idaho is home to a gigantic lake, Lake Pend Oreille, and a popular ski resort. On occasion, we drove up to the ski resort, from where we could look across the entire valley.

On the far side of the creek was a huge, fertile garden, which was my grandma's pride and joy. My grandpa helped to maintain the land, using his tractor to turn over the land. I loved to sit in the garden, with no agenda more pressing than to watch the raspberries as they changed color. When they hit perfect ripeness, I would harvest and eat them. There were so many that they provided a feast that lasted all summer.

The rest of the property, the part that my grandpa didn't manicure, was wild. There was dense forest and thickets of ferns, interspersed with paths my grandpa cut through the trees and shrubs for me to run around on. He used his trusty tractor to do this, this time trailing a brush hog attachment. Just below the mobile home, above the raspberry patch, he hung a swing from a couple of pine trees. I loved to sit on the swing, full of raspberries, and propel it as high as I could, singing songs to myself and enjoying the beautiful summer weather while my sisters played in the garden.

THEME: A SUMMER OF RESTORATION

The summer I spent with my grandparents in Idaho was idyllic. The weather was beautiful and, for the first time in my young life, I had few cares and worries. On Sue and Tom's Mountain and in Hyampom, there was always some form of stress or anxiety. We struggled to earn money, feed ourselves, and sustain our lives. Even when I wasn't directly involved in these challenges, I could feel the tension emanating from my mom and Pat. Our poverty influenced our lifestyle, our clothing, and our diet. At my grandparents' place, I was finally able to relax. All I needed to do was run around the woods, swing on the swing, and pick berries and apples.

My grandparents were retired or semiretired. I think my grandma worked part-time at the local Walmart. They took life easy and made me feel at home. It was a new experience for me, and one that helped me process some of the events of the previous few years. I stopped for a while, with no new challenges to address, and gathered myself physically, mentally, and spiritually.

The emotional stress of being taken away from my family took a toll on me that required more than a short break to heal. Over the course of several months, I internally pressed the reset button. It was as though the pressure of the previous years fell away from me and I was able to find a clean slate, ready to walk into the next phase of my life.

This period of **restoration** had few distinct episodes, which is why I've turned it into an interlude between larger chapters. Nonetheless, it was an important time. It was the first period in my life when I had the opportunity to experience the healing power of rest and relaxation, a lesson that later played an important role in my training philosophy.

AN IDAHO IDYLL

Grandma loved working in the garden. One of her favorite activities was pottering in her canning shed, which was full to the brim with canned products. I helped her as she harvested fruits and vegetables, prepared them for pickling, cooked them in a pressure cooker, and put them in jars.

My grandma was a collector of old bottles and, intriguingly, a world-class expert on antique jars. She loved to find and research old bottles and jars, and even wrote a book on the subject, compiling everything she knew about jar manufacturers of the nineteenth and twentieth centuries. The book contains pictures of the jars, along with information about where they were manufactured and by whom. The house was full of antique jars that she had recovered over the years: every counter and the top of every cabinet was covered with them. In later years, she received a lifetime achievement award for her books and her research into those particular types of antique bottles.

KETCHUP PICKLES SAUCES

19th CENTURY FOOD IN GLASS

by Betty Zumwalt

Oddly, my grandma was a world-class expert on antique bottles and jars. She wrote this comprehensive book on jars and jar manufacturers from the nineteenth and twentieth centuries.

My grandfather, on the other hand, based his life around his tractor and his tool shed. He liked nothing more than getting out and tilling the ground. Living where they did was the fulfillment of their long-held dream. They saved up and bought a plot of land well before retirement, worked on it until they had made it the way they wanted, and then retired there. For a boy who was used to living in natural surroundings, it was a familiar atmosphere. There were a few other houses visible in the distance, but we had no immediate neighbors. The house was surrounded by trees, the huge pond he had dug, a creek, and other foliage.

My grandpa loved to tell stories and jokes. He also loved to write poetry, even though none of his work was ever published. He simply wrote for his own amusement. He loved to sit around and read funny poems and jokes to my sisters and me. He was extremely hard of hearing, so to make him hear us we had to yell at him, even when he was wearing hearing aids.

Me and my sisters at our grandparents' house in Idaho, after they took us into custody.

STONEY COMES TO VISIT

At some point during the summer, my cousin Stoney and my great-grandmother came to visit us. Stoney and his mother were living with my great-grandmother at the time, helping to care for her.

I'd seen Stoney before. He lived in Sacramento with his mom, my aunt Susanne, and his older brother, John. During our time in California, my family and I occasionally visited them. When he came to my grandparent's house, however, Stoney looked very different than he did in Sacramento. He was dressed in nice clothes and seemed as though he was trying to behave well.

I recall John as a teenager who dropped out of school and was living away from home, sometimes on the streets. It was an open secret that he was working the streets as a prostitute in San Francisco. He liked my mom, so when we were in town, he stopped by to see her. One time, John tried to give my mom a beautiful diamond ring, but she wouldn't take it. She looked at him and told him that she knew he didn't have money, so the ring had to be stolen. I remember John getting angry and walking out of the room.

During our visits to Sacramento, John and Stoney would head out to the trees behind the property. A few times they dragged me along too. They pulled out cans with holes in them and sat there smoking weed. I thought this was unusual: I was used to seeing adults smoke weed, but I'd never seen kids smoking. I never took a hit, though. I just hung out with them while they got stoned, then we all returned to the house together.

John didn't come with my great-grandmother to visit my grandparents in Idaho, only Stoney. During his visit, we played in the garden, ran around the property, and picked raspberries. At the time, everything seemed calm and peaceful.

Little did I know it would be the last time I ever saw Stoney alive.

LESSON: THE IMPORTANCE OF RECOVERY

At the time, I couldn't have expressed the value of those blissful months in concrete terms. Now, I understand that adaptation to stress occurs in a cyclical fashion. When we train, our performance improves as we adapt to stress. Over time, however, if the stresses are too great or we don't incorporate sufficient recovery time, gains begin to diminish. To grow and adapt, we require stress, but equally, we need periods of rest and recovery. This is a delicate balance to strike: if we rest too frequently or for too long, we will become soft and move backward. We need stress to create adaptation.

The longer we stress the body for, the longer we need to rest. In the training world, we call this period supercompensation. First, we apply a huge amount of stress. As we accumulate fatigue, performance dips. Then, at the right time, we take a break and realize all the gains of that accumulated fatigue. Following supercompensation, performance rises to a higher level than it was prior to the rest.

This principle applies to all aspects of life. If we place ourselves under constant stress and deny ourselves recovery time, the body and mind will never truly adapt. If you burn the candle at both ends, year after year, after year, you cannot expect your performance to hold up, let alone to progress. Over time, you will see performance begin to degrade.

However busy your life is, make sure that you find time to properly recover. Otherwise your body, mind, and nervous system will pay the price.

FROM IDAHO TO OREGON

La Pine is a high desert ecosystem in central Oregon, situated at the edge of the Cascade Range of mountains. The area is a hotbed of volcanic activity that, over many millennia, has hollowed out numerous lake beds. This makes it a rich source of fish and an exceptionally popular fishing destination. People travel from miles around—even internationally—to seek out some of the best championship fishing in the world.

Pat's mother was in the hospital with cancer, from which she would never recover. This sad situation had just one silver lining: the cabin her husband had built before he passed away was, in the eyes of the state, a safe, stable living environment for my three sisters and me. When Pat and my mom moved into this cabin, they were able to prove that they could take care of us. They regained custody of me and my three sisters, and we moved with them to live in La Pine, although my brother stayed with his father in California.

Our parents drove out to Idaho to collect us and drive us back to Oregon. I accepted the change in my circumstances without question. As much as I loved living with my grandparents, it meant a great deal to me to be reunited with my closest family. By this time, the change in location hardly concerned me. I had already seen so many different places that I didn't care too much where we lived.

CHAPTER THREE

FUNCTIONAL AND DYSFUNCTIONAL RELATIONSHIPS

1986–1987 (AGE NINE TO TEN), LA PINE, CENTRAL OREGON

My father inherited two houses in Sonoma, California, in the heart of Wine Country. My grandfather and great-grandfather owned a large and successful concrete company. Their organization was involved in the construction of the Boulder Dam, now known as the Hoover Dam. Later, my grandfather lost his fortune on another project in Hawaii. Nonetheless, he was able to bequeath two houses in Sonoma to my father, who lived in one and rented out the other.

For the most part, my father didn't work. He occasionally

did some odd jobs, but mostly he lived off a disability allowance that he received from the state. His struggles with depression left him unable to hold a job. Sometimes, during the summer, I boarded the Greyhound bus and traveled from La Pine in Oregon to his home in California. He didn't drive, so I took the Greyhound into San Francisco, then changed to a series of regional buses to reach him in Sonoma.

When my dad was in good health, summers in Wine Country were phenomenal. Orange trees were so abundant that we could reach up and pull fresh oranges from their branches as we walked. The golden-brown hills, dotted with oak trees, were postcard perfect. Sonoma was blessed with hundreds of bike trails, so we rode around on our bikes visiting museums, stores, and the library. We usually found time to visit Sue and Tom's Mountain, where I reconnected with my friend Ganya.

We spent a lot of time at the library, seeking out practical books on how to make and do things. I borrowed a book on origami, and we spent many happy hours building as many different origami animals as we could. We researched go-karts and built one of our own, my dad taking me out and pushing me down some of the hills in the neighborhood, so I could build up a head of speed.

My dad loved to teach me about the things he enjoyed. For

example, he trained me to read and write in Morse code and use a Morse code transmitter. In the evenings, we listened to transmissions on his ham radio and deciphered what they said. He was fascinated by trains. He collected scale models and, on trips out, we always traveled by train if possible. We hiked the hills around Sonoma, exploring old limestone quarries and hanging out in groves of eucalyptus. The eucalyptus trees were originally planted as windbreaks, to protect crops growing in the area. I loved to hear them rustle and inhale their aroma as we hiked up the hills where they grew, in search of remote lakes.

Influenced by his time in a Tibetan monastery, my father was a Buddhist. His house was dotted with Buddhist statues and other artifacts of his faith. When I visited him, we often went to meetings where a facilitator led us in a guided meditation practice. My father was also attempting to conquer his alcoholism; he and I spent a lot of time together at Alcoholics Anonymous meetings while I was in town.

Ultimately, he sold both the houses he owned in Sonoma. The proceeds from the sale of one went toward his living expenses. The profits on the other he donated to a New Age guru, who was little more than a scam artist. He saved enough from the sales to purchase a condo in Santa Rosa, close to Sonoma, and the location of the hospital where I was born.

While the good visits with my dad were amazing, the bad ones were devastating. I remember visiting him in Santa Rosa and disembarking the bus at a store close to his new condo. It was my first visit to his new address, so I called him to come out and meet me. He told me he'd be right there. When I saw him, he was wearing sweatpants and a shirt. He had clearly been wearing the same clothes for weeks. I could see ring after ring of piss stains, indicating that he had been going to the bathroom in his clothes. His gait and the expression on his face looked strange. I could tell that he was happy to see me, but it was obvious something wasn't right.

When we got back to his condo, he called a taxi driver to buy him beer. I later found out that, by this time, none of the local stores would allow him to purchase alcohol, a restriction he sidestepped by hiring local cab drivers to buy booze and deliver it to him. It became clear that he was spending his days—his weeks—in a depressive state, lying in bed drinking.

Within a day or two of my arrival, it became clear that he was not going to sober up enough to take care of me or spend time with me while I was in town. He spent his entire time in bed, mumbling under the pillows when I bugged him to get up. After a couple of days, he got extremely drunk and depressed—I imagine he was disappointed in himself for the state he was in. He found some gasoline, poured it over himself, and stood outside his condo with a lighter in his hand, threatening to set himself on fire.

At this point, his neighbors intervened. He backed down, dropped the lighter, and eventually called his AA sponsor. When his sponsor arrived, it was obvious that my dad was in no state to take care of me. My dad made a few calls and I found myself staying with a friend of his for two weeks, hanging out with people I hardly knew, while—with the support of his sponsor—he struggled to get himself together.

I didn't tell my mom about the incident because I knew that if I did, I wouldn't be able to see my father again.

THEME: FUNCTIONAL AND DYSFUNCTIONAL RELATIONSHIPS

At this time, my relationships with family were the center of my life, for good or bad. I had no consistent home base, few friends, and no other real relationships. Family was the cornerstone of my life. While everything else around me seemed to be in constant flux, family was the anchor that enabled me to feel some sense of security and stability. Admittedly, that sense was sorely tested at times, notably when I was placed in foster care and I didn't know whether I'd ever see my parents and sisters again. Nonetheless, when the chips were down, the only people I could truly rely on were members of my family.

The stories in this chapter are primarily about **functional and dysfunctional relationships.** Without the relationships I had with members of my family, I wouldn't be the man I am today. My parents, siblings, and I were close, despite the dysfunctional elements of our relationships. Working together in the mountains forged strong bonds between us. We were always together. While Pat and my mom cultivated weed or chopped wood, I would take care of my siblings.

Some of the other relationships you'll read about in this chapter shaped me in a different way. They helped me understand who I wanted to become, and who I emphatically did *not* want to become. Through my relationships, I discovered what I value. That set of values has been an essential resource over the years, guiding my decisions and helping determine my purpose.

GROWING A DEEPER CONNECTION WITH MY STEPFATHER

The log cabin where we lived in Oregon contained an enormous open kitchen and living room, which gave us a lot of space to play with. One year, for example, we erected an enormous Christmas tree. It must have been fifteen or twenty feet tall.

La Pine is primarily a retirement community. The town is secluded and surrounded by tall trees, such as ponderosa and lodgepole pines, and well-known fishing lakes and rivers. Aside from some volcanic buttes, the area is flat, a major contrast from the mountainous terrain I was used to in California. Our new home was a log cabin, built by Pat's father, my step-grandfather.

My mother worked odd jobs such as cleaning houses. Pat wasn't working at the time, which was the first time I remember him being without a job. He took the opportunity to invest a lot of time in his relationship with me. My three sisters were his biological children, so you might imagine that he gave them more attention, but that wasn't the case. He told me that he had always wanted a son and that, in his eyes, I was his son, not merely his stepson. In fact, he revealed that he did have a son, from his first marriage, from whom he was totally estranged. He said that he had arrived home one day to find his wife and young son, Patrick Jr, gone. He didn't know where they were or how to find them.

One of the activities Pat and I enjoyed together was fishing. The rivers that flowed through and near La Pine were slow, beautiful, and meandering. They were also full of trout. Pat and I would get in our tan 1982 Toyota pickup and catch rainbow trout on the Little Deschutes River, which was just five minutes from where we lived.

In La Pine, my parents promised me that they were

done with growing weed. After Pat escaped from the cops in California, he succeeded in hiding out in the mountains and selling all the crops he had grown. They told me that my sisters and I were their priority and they weren't going to participate in any activities that would put the family in jeopardy. Before they made that break, however, they wrapped up activities in California and used the majority of the money to purchase that Toyota pickup. I was proud of my parents for owning such a nice vehicle. It had a canopy to keep the rain out and it was the first automobile we'd ever owned that was less than a decade old.

Over the course of the summer, Pat and I spent many happy hours fishing and talking about life. Pat taught me how to choose a good fishing spot, where to drop my line, and how to hide my shadow from the fish. Occasionally we captured crawdads, but the majority of our time was spent fishing.

When we weren't fishing, I enjoyed building and firing off model rockets. Pat and I went out into the woods behind our house, fired them high into the sky, and watched as they deployed their parachute and drifted slowly back down to earth. Most of the time we fired the rockets in areas that had been clear-cut for lumber, so there were few trees to snag them. Occasionally, however, one of them traveled further than we anticipated, floated into the woods, and got caught in the branches of a pine. We didn't mind, though; it was all part of the fun.

Pat was an interesting man. He could be warm and spontaneous, yet he was riddled with insecurities. In particular, he was terrified of losing his family. My mom's parents hated him and only visited us once the entire time we lived in La Pine. When they did, he was too scared to face them. He took his rifle, climbed a tree close to the house, and sat there, waiting, until they left.

To this day, I'm not sure what he was trying to achieve or who he sought to protect. I think he feared that they would try to take custody of me and my sisters. Seeing him up in the tree reminded me of the time he kept watch as the police approached our camp in Hyampom. On that occasion, his vigilance paid off. This time, it seemed unnecessary. My mom's parents were a sweet couple who treated the rest of the family kindly. For Pat, however, they had only disdain. I think the chaotic nature of our lives exacerbated normal friction, to the point where Pat and my mom's parents could hardly stand each other.

At times, Pat's insecurities verged on paranoia. If my mom's parents wanted to take custody of my sisters and me, the logical time to do so was when we were living with them. They never did that. For Pat, abandonment was a constant specter.

The family in La Pine, Oregon, after mom and Pat regained custody of us from our grandparents.

A BRIEF REUNION WITH MY BROTHER

While we lived in La Pine I saw Mark, my brother, for the first time in years. He came up from his father's place to visit us for a week. My mom briefed us beforehand that if he had a good time, he might want to move back with us.

During his visit, Mark and I played on the trails and in the woods, building forts among the pine trees. One of them was based on a huge, upturned pine stump. We laid branches of lodgepole pine against the back of the stump and filled in the gaps with pieces of bark from the various logs that lay around the woods. I vividly recall sitting in the fort with my brother, thinking how great it was to have him back and hoping that he would come live with us full time. I turned to him and said, "Ain't this the life? Everything's good and grand."

Unfortunately, Mark's father and stepmother suspected that we wanted him to move to La Pine with us. His stepmother, determined to prevent that from happening, convinced him to stand up in a custody hearing and tell the state Pat had sexually abused him while he stayed with us in La Pine. Mark was only around seven years old at the time, and he was vulnerable to his stepmother's manipulations.

Although I did visit Mark in California years later, that was the end of his involvement in my childhood. Both Pat and my mother were deeply resentful of the charges Mark's stepmother convinced him to level at the family. The lies Mark was manipulated into telling still haunt him to this day.

CORRESPONDENCE WITH MY FATHER

Although I rarely saw my father in person, we sustained a pen pal relationship throughout his life. It started while I lived in Hyampom, before I was old enough to write letters back. In lieu of writing, I drew pictures. I didn't have a lot of available paper, so I used the paper plates we ate off as a canvas. I cut my drawings into various shapes, stuffed them into envelopes, and sent them to my father.

While I lived in La Pine, I received regular postcards from him, detailing his travels to different parts of California. Although I enjoyed writing to him, it usually took me a long time to respond to his letters. I would start a letter, stop, and restart. Only a few times per year did I succeed in completing a letter and posting it to him. Nonetheless, this pen pal connection was our most consistent form of relationship all the way until his passing in 2002.

Having grown up with only intermittent access to electricity and the telephone, I have never gotten into the habit of calling people, even as an adult. Rarely do I speak to anyone on the phone. In La Pine I had access to one, but it didn't feel normal for me to pick up the phone and call my father. I felt much more comfortable writing letters. They gave me a way to feel connected to my father from a distance, even when I wasn't able to visit him due to his depression and alcoholism.

My mother played an important role in helping to maintain my relationship with my father. Despite our chaotic lifestyle and his troubled mind, she encouraged me to communicate with him and never said a bad word about him. Pat was largely supportive too, although he occasionally cracked jokes that hinted at his true feelings. My father, for all his struggles, made an enormous effort to stay in touch and let me know that he cared for me. I always felt that I was important to him.

Throughout my childhood, I watched Pat and my mom spend their evenings drinking and smoking weed, sometimes joined by friends. While we lived in La Pine, my mom's relationship with alcohol began to deteriorate. One evening, the two of them were drinking together when they got into an argument. My mom became so enraged that she started picking up kitchen knives and throwing them full force at Pat, with the intention of killing him. Pat ran around the kitchen dodging the knives and attempting to hide behind the centerpiece of our open-plan kitchen and living room. In desperation, he yelled at her to stop because I was in the room and yelled at me to do something, anything, to calm her down.

I remember a feeling of powerlessness. My mom was strong and athletic and disarming her seemed impossible. Moreover, Pat was always adamant that no amount of provocation justified a physical response to a woman. Even in such desperate circumstances, he was unwilling to lay a finger on my mom. The scene continued until she ran out of knives to throw, at which point she finally began to calm down. My mother of course doesn't remember this, or many episodes that took place while she was drinking, as she was blackout drunk by this time.

It was the first time I had ever seen my mother exhibit such violent rage, and I struggled to understand what had happened. Why didn't Pat respond? Why didn't he attempt to restrain her when he was at risk of serious injury or death? Unfortunately, it wouldn't be the last time Pat and my mother's relationship degenerated into alcohol-fueled violence.

BREAKING MY ARM, BUT FEELING NO PAIN

When we moved to La Pine, I started the fourth grade. Initially, I struggled to make friends. I was very quiet and not particularly sociable, especially in large groups. My first year in La Pine, I didn't have any friends at all. During lunch time I used to play on the swing alone. My detached behavior worried Pat and my mom so much that they connected with the parents of another kid, who also didn't have many friends, to set up a playdate.

By the time I reached fifth grade, I began to play more with other kids. During winter, for example, a group of us went out during lunch breaks and built giant snowballs together. There was a camaraderie in being part of a group and playing together that I enjoyed.

During the spring, we played another, albeit more dangerous, game. The game went like this. One kid got on the floor to lay on his back, with his legs bent and his feet cocked. Another kid climbed onto his feet, held in place by several others. The kid on the floor then pushed with all their strength, throwing them as high into the air as possible.

When it was my turn, I got up on a kid's feet and found myself thrown far into the air. I felt as if I was flying. That feeling soon ended and as the ground rushed toward me, I thrust out my arm to break my fall. Bam! I felt the impact and heard one of the bones in my arm break.

I got up and when I told them what had happened, a lot of the kids around me started to freak out. To calm them down, I remained cool and collected. "It's okay. I broke my arm. I'll go see the nurse."

As I wandered into the school nurse's office, I held the broken arm with my opposite hand.

"What's going on?" she said.

"I broke my arm," I told her.

She looked at me strangely. "No, no you didn't."

"I did. I broke it right here." I pointed to the place where I could feel the break.

The nurse still wasn't convinced. "No," she said. "No, you didn't break your arm."

A little exasperated, I tried to show her the break. "It's right here. Can't you see where it's swelling?"

"You probably sprained it. If you'd broken it, you'd be crying."

We went back and forth for a while longer when I finally told her I needed to call my mom. My mom picked me up and took me to the doctor's office. Sure enough, my arm was broken, exactly where I felt it break.

You might think the nurse should have listened to me, but I understand her response. I walked into her office, perfectly calm, and told her I had broken my arm. A perfectly calm fifth grader with a broken arm wasn't a sight she saw every day. For me, chaos was a part of daily life. Breaking my arm didn't seem like a big deal. I also didn't feel any pain.

The doctor set my arm in a cast and my mom took me home. She wanted me to take ibuprofen; I chose to drink a Coke instead. The next day, I was back at school.

It wasn't until I was in my thirties that I discovered I actually have a disorder of the nervous system. My sensitivity to pain is very low; some I don't even feel. This disorder was diagnosed several surgeries later in life, as it became apparent that my responses were highly unusual. Obviously as a kid, I knew none of this.

Breaking my arm posed other challenges, mainly because I broke the arm I used to write. I tried to write with my left hand, but it didn't work out. A friend of mine ended up helping me with all my writing while my arm was broken. Unfortunately, I have almost no memory of him; I don't even remember his name.

PAT'S FINAL ESTRANGEMENT FROM HIS SIBLINGS

Pat rarely spoke about the rest of his family. I heard little about them throughout my childhood and following the death of his mother, which happened while we were living there, he never spoke of them again. While we were living in La Pine, however, as it became clear that his mother was losing her battle to cancer, he began to talk about them. Presumably, he was in discussions with them about how to handle her impending death, which brought them to the forefront of his consciousness. It was plain to me that he saw his siblings and their families as urban and pretentious, in stark contrast to our rural, self-reliant existence.

His brothers were attorneys and accountants, roles which Pat evidently found highly distasteful. He mocked them because they didn't work with their hands, and because they supposedly wore silk underwear. This was a major point for him, a symbol of their apparent degeneracy. The more he discussed them, the more obvious it was that he respected physical work. In many ways, Pat's sensibilities lay in the arts. He loved to read and write. Despite this inclination, he believed strongly in the value of work. It was important to him that I developed practical skills. Among other useful skills, he taught me how to hunt, fish, take apart and clean a gun, sharpen a knife and a chain saw, and split wood quickly and efficiently. His father, he said, had won a Golden Gloves trophy as a military boxing champion. The same man had built the house we occupied at the time. It was clear that these were achievements Pat recognized and valued.

Shortly after her death, Pat's siblings arrived and began to divvy up her possessions, seemingly oblivious to Pat's wishes. There was a lot to divvy up. Pat's mother liked to collect things and had an entire room full of brand-new appliances. They were unused, still in their boxes. She was a woman who loved to shop and had the means to do so. Her affluence was reflected in the décor of the house: the main living and dining area was lit by an enormous chandelier.

Not everything in the house belonged to Pat's mother,

but his siblings behaved as though it was all fair game. One of them walked into my room and told me he was going to take my pillows. I tried to explain that the pillows were mine—we had bought them ourselves—but he refused to listen. In his eyes, anything in his mother's home belonged to him.

Pat didn't fight him. Quite the opposite, actually. He told me to let him have the pillows. It soon became clear that Pat found the whole situation despicable and had already made a decision to have no part of it. After his siblings had left, he gathered the family together and told us we were moving. "They're taking the house," he said. "They're splitting everything." He viewed what was happening as ugly and demeaning, and the only way he knew how to handle that was to get as far away from it as possible. Pat wanted no part of this transaction and, it turned out, no further interaction with any members of his family. After we left La Pine, I never saw any of them again.

I spent a lot of time attempting to reconcile Pat's love of family with his attitude toward his siblings. He came from a large family—he had at least five brothers and sisters, maybe more—and he was the youngest. Everything he had taught me, everything I had experienced, told me that family was sacred. It was our one anchor in a confusing and sometimes hostile world. Pat was so committed to this belief that he never allowed me to refer to my sisters as half-sisters. In his world, there was only family. My sisters were my sisters. He was my father. I was his son.

Simultaneously, however, he was willing to separate from his blood relatives, telling me that I didn't need to know who they were because they would never be part of my life. To me, this seemed like a paradox. If family was so important, how could he sever all communication with his siblings? My one experience meeting them was in the wake of his mother's death, and despite their apparent greed, I had no other context to judge their characters. Admittedly, they didn't present themselves in a positive fashion. On the other hand, the death of a parent brings a lot of emotion to the surface. It can bring out the worst in people. I'll never know how the relationship deteriorated so badly that they felt able to walk into our home and treat us with total disrespect.

LESSON: THE POWER OF RELATIONSHIP

Relationships are the cornerstone of every element of life: from family, to social life, to business. A lot of people pay lip service to the value of relationships in business without truly understanding how essential they are to success—and how satisfying it is to build strong, trusting relationships. Relationships are the fun part of life. It's tempting to become caught up in entrepreneurial ideas and technical progress, only to forget that it is our relationships that put a smile on our face and give our work meaning.

Real relationships take work. Your decisions about which relationships to invest in could be the single greatest determinant of your happiness and success. The best relationships in our lives help us become more than we are, perhaps even more than we believe we can be. Achieving these kinds of results takes commitment to seeing and bringing out the best in one another.

Sometimes, building life-enhancing relationships requires difficult conversations. It's not enough to stay on the surface and skirt around our true emotions. In my relationship with my biological father, there were many occasions when I saw his pain and despair in close quarters. It was, at times, a heartbreaking experience. Yet, I always knew that we were committed to each other. We had conversations that caused me to question my deepest beliefs and reassess my path in life.

We also argued. When I saw him behaving in a way that I felt was detrimental to his health or didn't meet his ambitions for who he could be, I told him so. It's difficult to argue respectfully, and it takes a lot of emotional strength. By definition, due to the sheer energy involved, it's a commitment reserved for a few people in our lives.

You'll meet many people in your life and career with whom you don't feel such a strong connection. For whatever reason, you're not drawn to invest in them. Perhaps you feel that, if you do, the investment will be one-sided. Perhaps their interests are different from your own. Perhaps you get along on a surface level, but don't feel drawn to dive in more deeply. That's okay. Discernment is a key part of cultivating healthy relationships.

There may be times when you need to cut people out of your life because staying connected to them is dragging you down or leading you in a direction in which you don't wish to travel. That's okay too. Whatever you want to accomplish in life, relationships are the vehicle that will get you there. Make sure that you surround yourself with people who want to see you succeed, and who you want to see succeed. Ensure that your values match. Invest your energy wisely.

Having read these first few chapters, you might be questioning the values Pat and my mother lived by. They grew weed, which was illegal at the time, and it was a choice that had painful consequences for the entire family. Nonetheless, they lived by their own unshakable moral code. Family was their top priority in life. They cherished self-reliance and hated to feel that they were indebted to anyone. They strove to deliver value in the world, whether that was through baking pies, chopping down wood, or performing some other task.

My mom refused to take a diamond ring from my cousin John when she suspected it was stolen. She told Pat that they could only be together if he stayed away from hard drugs. Her choices may not match your own personal values, but they emanated from a strong set of beliefs about right and wrong.

By way of contrast, consider Pat's siblings. While he broke the law, they were all law-abiding people, many of them in respected professions. Yet, they did nothing to support their mother while she was battling cancer. When she died, they arrived to take whatever they could from her estate. For all his faults, Pat was incredibly loyal. He made sure to remind me at every turn that he saw me as his son, irrespective of whether we were related by blood. When his siblings showed up and started to raid his dead mother's property, he preferred to go into the unknown than stay and participate in behavior that he considered undignified and demeaning.

Whose values are right? That's not for me to tell you. What I can tell you is that making sure I have the right people in my life has been absolutely essential to my success in both business and life. I surround myself with people who share my vision and values, and—in the alchemy that we create together—amazing things occur. I encourage you to think very carefully about who you invest in, and who you ask to invest in you. Relationships are the rocket fuel that propels you along your chosen path.

FROM LA PINE TO WHERE?

We packed as many of our belongings as we could fit into our tiny Toyota pickup, piled in, and hit the road. The Toyota was a tiny two-seater with a small bed and a canopy in the back. My three sisters and I climbed into the back and rolled around as the vehicle bumped along the road into the desert.

As we rolled out of La Pine, I had no idea what to expect. The previous two years, first with my grandparents in Sand Point and then with my family in La Pine, were two of the most stable years of my childhood. I lived in a safe, warm environment, surrounded by care. Then, suddenly, it was time to move on. I didn't know where we were going, but it seemed a safe bet that it wouldn't be nearly as comfortable as our cozy cabin in La Pine.

Despite this premonition, I felt no anxiety or sense of foreboding. Deep in my heart, I trusted that we would survive and do fine, no matter what happened to us. I was certain that we would face new environments, new circumstances, and new challenges. Equally, I felt a sense of readiness. Following my interlude with my grandparents, I was excited for a new adventure.

I remember as we drove past the sagebrush, watching herds of antelope grazing in the distance. If they could survive in such a harsh environment, I felt sure that my family could meet whatever came our way.

CHAPTER FOUR

PERSEVERANCE

1987–1989 (AGE TEN TO TWELVE), PAULINA, OREGON

The trailer we lived in when we moved to Paulina was originally only intended for camping in the summer. It cost $375 and measured sixteen feet in length. It served us reasonably well when we moved in during our second summer in the area, but by the following winter, it was a different story.

Most of eastern Oregon is a desert. Prineville, the closest town to where we settled in Paulina, is a farming and ranching community on an open plain, dotted with homesteads from the 1800s and early 1900s.

Over the years, the area had been subject to significant logging. As we drove through the mountains, we saw big swathes of territory that had been logged out, along with some areas where only the largest trees had been removed and the rest remained, testimony to the ways in which logging methods had evolved over the years.

We were about forty-five minutes out of Prineville, in the Ochoco Mountain range, nestled among big, beautiful ponderosa pines and firs. Our sixteen-foot trailer was located next to a small stream, by the side of a road leading deeper into the mountains. It was winter, and the stream was completely frozen.

The area was formed by volcanic activity. The stream and the road wound through a ravine heading up into the mountains while on either side, the mountains jutted up exceptionally fast, creating a wall of rock by the side of the creek and right across the road.

In eastern Oregon, the many mountain ranges capture most of the precipitation as the clouds come off the coast. Most of the rain and snow falls over the mountains and central Oregon. By the time the clouds reach eastern Oregon, the clouds have dropped the majority of their payload. Outside our trailer, the ground was covered in only four to six inches of snow. Without cloud cover, however, the temperature plummeted. It was extremely cold.

Six of us—Pat, my mom, my three sisters, and me—huddled around propane heaters in our sixteen-foot trailer. You may struggle to visualize how small a sixteen-foot trailer really is, so allow me to paint a picture. There was one dining room table that seated three people. The table could be pushed down, and the seats rolled out so that it became a small bed, smaller than the average twin-sized bed. That's where my sisters slept.

Next to the dining table stood a mini stove, a mini sink, and a mini fridge. The fridge was roughly a foot high and a foot deep, about the same size as an Igloo freezer—the kind you may have used on a camping outing.

In the back of the trailer was the bed where my parents slept. It was technically a double, although it wasn't full length. Above my parents' bed was another platform, and that's where I slept. There was no bathroom or shower in the trailer.

With the six of us, there was nowhere to go, nowhere to sit. My parents sat on the bed. My sisters and I squeezed around the three-person dining table. We had two options: stand up or sit down. There was no space to do anything more.

The platform I slept on creaked and rattled with every move I made, disturbing my parents and my sisters. Every time I rolled over, they complained. For a couple of nights,

I tried not to move, which was extremely stressful. I found it difficult to fall asleep and, when I did, I inevitably moved, causing the bed to creak loudly.

It was so bad that my parents eventually told me to go sleep in the back of our Toyota pickup. At first, I thought this was a good solution, until I realized how cold it was outside. I had one thin sleeping bag that I climbed into, with another one laid on top of me, but that wasn't enough. The sleeping bags weren't suitable for sleeping outside in such biting temperatures. We had found them at the Salvation Army used-goods store or inherited them from people who no longer needed them. Every night, my toes froze, and I shivered as I slept. When I complained to my parents, they gave me an extra blanket and told me I'd be fine. After that, I dealt with the cold as best I could.

During the day, there was nothing to do in the trailer but read books, so that's how we spent our winter, huddled in our sixteen-foot trailer, reading. I also went out and hiked the frozen creek, walking for miles in either direction. Sometimes I pretended I was skating, sliding first on one foot, then the other, as far as I could go.

THEME: LEARNING TO PERSEVERE

Living in Paulina was a difficult time for our family. We were scraping by, barely making ends meet, attempting to put our lives back together after leaving La Pine. It was also a difficult time for me personally, as I struggled with the cold and with the feeling of being a social outcast.

As painful as it was to feel the lack of acceptance from my schoolmates, however, I never allowed myself to give up and allow their negative perceptions to define me. On the contrary, the hardship brought out grit and **perseverance** in me, as it did in the rest of my family. No matter what happened, no matter how tough our circumstances became, my parents never gave up. They kept putting one foot in front of the other, attempting to make good things happen. They faced setback after setback, yet they picked themselves up, came up with a new approach, and strove to move forward.

In difficult times, we may not be able to fall back on comfort. When times are hard and we long for something better, perseverance may be the only thing we can fall back on. All we can do is resist the temptation to give in and reach out in search of charity, figure out how to make our situation better, and then do the work that will ultimately bring us success. In the darkest times, perseverance is an indispensable ally.

REBUILDING OUR LIVES IN PAULINA

When my family first left La Pine, Pat succeeded in

securing a job logging timber in the Ochoco Mountains. These mountains are around three hours' drive from La Pine, which is located in the central corridor of Oregon. As we traveled east, away from the mountains and the sea, some regions of mountainous terrain rose out of the desert. The Ochoco Mountains is one of these.

It was summer when we moved. We set up our camping trailer in the mountains, and Pat went out logging while my mom and us kids explored the area. Before long, I noticed that when Pat arrived home, he was exhausted and in a lot of pain. I saw that he strapped up his wrist with a brace before he left for work every morning. I asked what was wrong and he admitted that he was finding it difficult to keep up with the younger men with whom he was working. "I can out cut them," he said, "but keeping up with them around the hillsides is proving a real challenge." Pat's boss was all over him for his lack of speed and, within a few weeks, he was let go.

Shortly after he lost the logging job, Pat told me that his arm was broken. He broke it before I was born, perhaps ten or fifteen years earlier. He had been living in California, working for a private contractor digging out swimming pools. The firm built pools located in tight spaces, where it was impossible to bring in excavators, so Pat and his coworkers were responsible for digging these pools by hand with shovels.

While he was doing this job, he broke his arm at the wrist. Although he went to a hospital and had his arm placed in a cast, he needed to get back to work as soon as possible. He waited until he thought the arm was healed, cut the cast off, and went back to work. Unfortunately, the bones in his arm had not fully mended. They moved back and forth as he worked, wearing a gap between the ends of the two fractured bones.

He could hardly have picked a worse profession to grit his teeth and power through with a broken wrist. The chain saw he used for logging required a lot of strength and sent painful vibrations through his arm while he worked. He did it because he needed to make a living and take care of his family. Unfortunately, the state of his arm gradually became untenable. In the Ochocos, it became obvious that he couldn't continue to work in logging.

Pat losing his job was our cue to make a move out of the Ochocos. Initially, we headed into the nearby town of Paulina, located about an hour further east of Prineville. Prineville had a population in the region of five thousand. Paulina consisted of a small general store, a one-room schoolhouse, and little else. To reach our favorite resource, the public library, we needed to make the hour's journey into Prineville.

When we realized that the area was rich in semiprecious

gemstones, we began educating ourselves on the subject. The region had a rich geological history and had been home to rich agate beds, along with deposits of petrified wood, jasper, thunder eggs, and fossils. Most of these were mined or removed decades before our arrival, but we used to enjoy wandering a short distance out of town and picking up the few shards we could find.

While the pickings were minimal, our location piqued my parents' interest in geology. With a library in the area, they took the opportunity to research the local geology and learn about the extensive deposits of semiprecious minerals close to our home. Pat and my mom loved to read and were always researching some new interest. The combination of living in Paulina and having access to a lot of information about the geology of the area sparked their curiosity into life. They learned about agate, jasper, and thunder eggs—the state rock of Oregon.

Thunder eggs were formed when Oregon was an underwater seabed. Volcanic vents bubbled beneath the surface, infusing the mud and clay of the sea floor with bubbles of air. Over time, these bubbles filled with a rocky substance named rhyolite, which formed the thunder egg's outer core. Then, agate and other minerals leeched into the "egg," filling the hollow center and creating the thunder eggs that would be discovered around Prineville millions of years later. Janis and my mom continue to mine them to this day.

As our interest in geology grew, we took advantage of the warm weather to relocate up into the Ochocos. We spent most of that summer researching, hiking, and digging. Most of the dig sites near Paulina and the Ochocos were exhausted in the 1960s and '70s, so there wasn't much for us to excavate. With Pat unable to work in logging, our income was minimal.

Geographically, Paulina was an interesting area. It was a plateau, surrounded by valleys. In the valleys, perhaps a thousand feet below the plateau, were rivers, grassland, and a ranching community. The uncultivated land was mostly sagebrush.

Like Hyampom, Paulina was barely a town. It consisted of a general store, a rarely used community hall, and a two-room schoolhouse. It was a place where ranchers and their families could pick up supplies without needing to drive an additional hour into Prineville, and for kids up to eighth grade to go to school and get an education. The ranching community was spread far and wide across the grassland, so although the population was small, Paulina served people from far afield.

The owner of the general store offered to rent us a small

house behind the store, which became our home base. One of the areas we liked to dig was in the Ochoco Mountains called Whistler Springs, which was an old thunder egg dig site. The site had already undergone decades of digging, mostly by day diggers. This meant that there were still numerous treasures to be mined at a deeper level.

Our *modus operandi* was to find an old, disused hole and dig down further than anyone had previously gone. Alternatively, we looked for trees or tree stumps and dug close to the roots, where fewer people had dug previously. The first fifteen or twenty feet were overfill—dirt that had been moved from hole to hole over the years. Below that depth, we had a real chance of finding thunder eggs. We spent a month out in Whistler Springs, digging deeply into the ground and pulling out thunder eggs to sell.

Unfortunately, Pat had another accident. He was twenty-five feet down in a hole, digging for thunder eggs, when he hit a hollow one with his pickax. The thunder egg exploded into flames, filling the entire hole with thick, acrid smoke as it burned out. We'll never know exactly what was in the center of the thunder egg. Whatever it was, Pat climbed out of the hole hacking and wheezing, and spent the next week shaking and sweating in bed. After that, we closed our digging season and returned to Paulina. We settled in for the winter and I returned to school.

Pat remained sick for months. Although he went to see the doctor numerous times, we never understood exactly what was in the smoke he had inhaled. The effects, however, were permanent. Pat sustained permanent damage to his lungs, to the extent that any physical activity made it hard for him to breathe. He became asthmatic and began using an inhaler.

Despite Pat's diminished physical condition, life in Paulina was initially relatively comfortable. We had electricity, television, and heating. Admittedly, the TV could only receive one station, and even then, the picture was sketchy. To watch *Wheel of Fortune* and *Jeopardy*, we had to adjust the antenna to precisely the right position to reduce the snowy screen.

As we were in a ranching area, stalls housing cattle surrounded our little home on three sides. This meant that we lived with the constant stench of cattle dung and made us vulnerable to infestations of horseflies. Nonetheless, we were quite happy. We were warm, dry, and the property was incredibly cheap.

BATTLING THE COLD

Out on the plateaus of eastern Oregon, it doesn't snow much; the clouds dump all their precipitation before traveling so far inland. Our first winter in Paulina, we saw about an inch of snow. It does, however, get incredibly cold.

Prior to Christmas, I went to school in dirty clothes, with my shoes so worn that they were falling off my feet. I typically picked shoes at Goodwill and wore them until my toes poked through the deteriorating leather.

Everyone in the community knew that we were dirt poor, so several people got together to present my parents with boxes of food. I think some people even donated cash. I loved their thoughtfulness. My parents, however, were extremely upset. They said that we could get along on our own and that they didn't want our family to accept charity. We didn't ask for the food or money, so they found the whole thing insulting and returned the donations.

They may have made it harder to get by, but they wanted to feel that they were working for whatever they had. Even so, we did access some level of government support in the form of food stamps and other programs. Without that, we would have been unable to survive at times.

Over Christmas break, the temperature was so low that the oil inside our oil tank froze. This tank contained the oil we used to power the oil heater that warmed our house. For it to freeze, the temperature must have dropped as low as -40 or -50 degrees. Our landlord brought over an electric blower heater to thaw out the oil heater, and still it took about a week before the oil thawed enough for us to turn on the heat. We were without heat for approximately three weeks in -40-degree weather.

While we waited for our oil heater to become usable again, I went out to look for tiny pieces of wood we could burn. Pat was still incapacitated from his illness, so it was down to me to do what I could to provide the house with heat. With hardly a tree or shrub to be seen on the grassland surrounding Paulina, I resorted to seeking out old fence posts and chipping them into tiny pieces.

There was a small gap in the front of the oil heater, intended for people to reach in and light it. We stuffed these tiny chips of wood into the heater, lit them, and used them as our only source of heat. In effect, we jerry-rigged the oil heater to serve as a wood-burning stove.

During the weeks our oil heater was out of commission, the temperature inside the house was probably below zero. This meant that the water lines were also frozen. The temperature was so low that, after Christmas, when it warmed up to -7 degrees, it felt warm to me. The sun was out, there were no clouds, and I went out on my bike and rode around in short sleeves.

When my sisters and I played outside during the winter,

we didn't have appropriate clothing. We played in the snow in jeans. Sometimes we went up into the mountains and did some sledding, wearing no more than jeans and tennis shoes. We used socks as gloves. By the time we finished playing, our fingers and toes were completely numb, but we didn't think anything of it. It seemed normal.

As winter faded away and spring began, grass began to sprout in the yard. It grew quickly; soon it was roughly a foot tall. We had no lawnmower, so I improvised. I found an old, two-handled scythe and chopped down the grass on our half-acre of lawn by hand. Again, it seemed normal. I got the job done and got a good workout. It was only later in life, looking back, that I realized how unusual my experience of childhood was.

MAKING A LIVING WITHOUT BEING PART OF THE WORLD

As our first winter in Paulina passed and spring began to roll around, my parents continued to research the geography of the area. They discovered more places close to home that had the potential to yield valuable minerals. They both became quite passionate about this hobby and possible income stream, especially my mother, who was the primary driving force in the relationship. I think she enjoyed being on the right side of the law. She didn't need to grow weed to make ends meet. Instead, she was engaged in something she liked and attempting to turn it into a small business.

Like most of my childhood, our time in Paulina was undoubtedly a time of financial insecurity. However, it was also a time of optimism. We were putting in the groundwork to develop a sustainable source of income. Over spring break, we set up camp and tarps and dug for agate. We also began hunting for fossils and petrified trees.

Petrification happens when, over millions of years, all the organic material is replaced by minerals. While the main body of a tree will become petrified, cracks and crevices in the branches may be filled with silica that eventually solidifies into agate—a translucent variety of microcrystalline quartz that forms in a range of attractive colors. This process is known as a limb cast and produces some stunning agate specimens. At first glance, they appear clear. In a certain light, however, they reveal a pink hue.

Inside the agate, dendrites—a mineral formation that looks like a black exploding star—sometimes forms. Other specimens may contain moss agate, which occurs when cracks in the stone are filled with other minerals. Moss agate gets its name because it looks as though multicolored moss is growing inside the stone. When it's cut open, it can be used to produce gorgeous jewelry.

On one occasion, we found an entire petrified tree laying out in the wild, with branches sprouting off it. We pulled off the pieces we wanted, then buried it again to save the rest of it for the next season.

Although we didn't have the tools to process any of the stones we found, we began to collect them. My mom picked up a buffing wheel that she used to start polishing what we had, and we made friends with a miner who worked up in the mountains. He cut up some of what we brought back from our excursions. Ultimately, my mom's goal was to make and sell jewelry. We weren't sure how we'd reach that goal, but we took every practical step we could afford toward making it a reality.

I loved looking for limb casts. The area where we found the best minerals was close to a river that cut through the land, running through some rolling hills that provided relief from the flat of the plains. The spring was the best time to go and look for new pieces of agate. The fresh rain softened up the land and stripped a layer from the ground, making it easier to see what minerals might be lying just below the surface.

I went out for an entire day at a time, roaming the hills with my backpack in search of cool pieces. Once I found a giant block of agate, perhaps ten or fifteen feet around, surrounded by a clay structure that had hardened into concrete. The petrified tree limbs running through it had an outer core of agate and a solid, black, mineral inner core. The inner core had agatized a little around the edges, so I was able to break a few of them off. In later years, I turned some of them into art pieces.

HUNTING AND FORAGING

While we lived in the Paulina area, we spent our summers camping out in the Ochocos. As we did in Hyampom, we foraged for mushrooms as a fun and cheap way of locating food. One of my favorites was a variety named shaggy mane, which grew abundantly in gravelly areas by the side of the road. We often kept a cooler in the truck and, when we spotted a patch of shaggy mane, we jumped out, harvested them, and threw them in the cooler. They tasted delicious fried. We ate them as a side dish almost every day.

Another of my favorites was the puffball. These mushrooms came in two varieties: the regular puffball and the pineapple puffball. The pineapple puffball had a split in the top and a series of grooves down the side, making it look similar to a pineapple. Both usually grew within a hundred yards of a stream, and they could reach up to a foot in diameter. As their name suggests, puffballs were prone to exploding. If we attempted to harvest them too late, they popped open in a haze of dust and spores. The trick was to catch them when they were big enough to eat, but not so large that they were ready to explode. We sliced them up, picked out the bugs—certain types of beetle loved burrowing into puffballs—and fried them, either plain or breaded. The fried slices were almost as big as a pancake.

One of my regular morning activities was to head out into the fields to catch grasshoppers. Then, I went down to a stream, fed them onto a hook, and used them for fishing. My favored section of stream was a couple of miles long. It meandered through a valley named Bear Creek, where we frequently camped. Although it was only a couple of feet wide, there were places where trees had fallen across the stream, creating natural dams. This led to the formation of large pools of water.

The water was so clear that fish could easily see me as I cast my line into the stream. To avoid spooking them, I used to hide behind a tree or bush close to the bank. Alternatively, I would cast upstream to one of the pools, allowing the current to suck my bait downstream where the fish gathered. I spent many long summer days walking and fishing, starting at one end of the stream and working my way down through the valley. By the end of the day, I usually succeeded in catching at least half a dozen brook trout, sometimes as many as a dozen. I gutted them, skinned them, and took them home so we could eat them for dinner.

Although I was still a little young to hunt, I occasionally went out with Pat while he poached a deer. My task was to help him gut the deer rapidly, so that we could get out of the woods before the forest service or the police caught up with us. After Pat shot the animal, we gutted it, skinned it, butchered it, and buried the innards right where we were. Then we wrapped the chunks of meat, tossed them into a backpack, and threw the backpack in the back of our truck. This was a rare occurrence because it was so risky, but there were times when we needed to get some bigger meat on the table, and we didn't have the money to buy any.

In between these sporadic deer hunts, we shot rabbits and pheasants. Both were prevalent in the area and provided good eating. I developed a huge collection of lucky rabbits' feet, souvenirs of dozens of successful hunts. Another animal that made its way onto our table was porcupine. They're slow-moving creatures, generally found in trees, so they were easy to corner. What we didn't realize, until we tried to kill one, was that porcupines are incredibly resilient animals. The first time we shot and injured a porcupine, it refused to die. A slug from our .22 rifle wasn't powerful enough to penetrate the skull of a porcupine. We found that the only way we could see them off was to club them to death.

Porcupines didn't make for the best eating, but they were

better than going hungry. They had to be skinned immediately, because if they sat in their skin for any length of time, their meat would become tainted. As you can imagine, skinning a porcupine was a tricky task. As I did with the rabbits' feet, I collected the quills, claws, and teeth of porcupines.

FRIENDSHIPS AND SCHOOLING

I had a few friends in Paulina. There were a couple of other kids in town who I played with. I had a small bike that my parents had picked up used: we took it to the hills close to town and rode it down at breakneck speed, making jumps and pulling other stunts. Usually, we crashed and ended up injuring ourselves.

This was also a time when I first immersed myself in learning. Our school consisted of two rooms. First through fourth grades were in the first room, while fifth through eighth grades were taught in the second room. I was in fifth and sixth grade while we lived in Paulina, so I was part of the second group.

There were three people in my year, making it the most densely populated age group in the entire school. Most grades contained only one or two kids. The school only catered to children up to eighth grade, so those who were in high school took the bus into Prineville, an hour's drive away. The bus driver collected all the students in the morning, ferried them to school, hung out in Prineville all day long, and then drove them back in the afternoon.

All the kids between fifth and eighth grade were taught by the same teacher, although he didn't do a lot of teaching. He was sick with cancer and was slowly dying. In the mornings, he wrote a schedule up on the board, detailing what he wanted us to do over the course of the day. For example, he might set us the task of working through an English lesson between 8 a.m. and 9 a.m., followed by some math problems from 9 a.m. to 10 a.m. Then he sat behind his desk and fell asleep. There was a shelf in the room that contained the books pertaining to each different grade. We were expected to find the relevant books and study quietly.

Over the course of sixth grade, I worked through every single book, in every discipline, all the way through high school. I completed every workbook, quiz, and activity, along with every available extracurricular exercise. At the end of a typical textbook was a series of multiple-choice questions, some essay topics, and some extracurricular work. I worked through every single one. It wasn't until later, when I went to high school, that I discovered that students were expected to select from the questions on offer, rather than tackling every single one. Learning fired me up. I devoured every scrap of information I could find, just because I was interested.

Pushing myself, in any endeavor, came naturally to me. In the evenings, if I got bored, I went behind the school and ran laps, until I couldn't run any more.

SUMMER IN THE MOUNTAINS

By the beginning of our second summer in Paulina, we could no longer afford to live in the small house behind the general store. The weather was good, so we took our trailer up into the mountains, set up camp, and spent our days mining and collecting rocks. With no shower facilities, we bathed outside. We took gallon jugs down to a nearby creek, filled them, and let them sit on a rock all day to heat up in the sunlight. When the water was warm enough, we stood on the rocks and poured it over our heads to shower.

Over the course of that summer, we got to know some of the people who regularly visited the mountains. They were hunters, fishermen, and people who came to see what they could dig out of the mining claims. Pat and my mom hung out with them, drinking and showing them some of the prettiest thunder eggs we had collected. These were the ones that had been cut up for us by our friend who worked as a miner, and which my mom or Pat had polished. Our guests were impressed, and I recall thinking that we were about to sell some of them, turning a small profit on all our hard work.

What usually happened, however, was that my parents gave the thunder eggs away as gifts. I was perplexed. Didn't they realize that the potential market for these minerals was small? We were dirt poor. We couldn't afford to give away our few assets. Yet we did. I never understood how my parents could be so adamant on rejecting charity, but willing to give away minerals they could have sold to supplement our meager income.

The summer came to a close and the new school year began. We still didn't have a permanent place to call home and no visible source of income—the mining and selling of minerals hadn't progressed beyond the level of a hobby. Recognizing this, my mom decided to train as a registered nursing assistant (RNA) at a college a few towns away. She also interned part time as a nursing assistant as she trained. She kept this job for a while, until she realized that it was out of alignment with her principles. At that point, she quit, a move that was also the catalyst for the family to leave Paulina.

While my mom was training, she dropped me off early in the morning with friends in Prineville, who took me to school with their kids while she went to school and work. To me, Prineville seemed enormous. It wasn't— even today the population is only around 9,000—but to a boy raised mainly in the wilderness, its size felt astronomical.

This was the toughest time. At night, I froze in the back of our pickup. By day, I felt isolated and ostracized. Going to school in Prineville was a huge culture shock for me. In La Pine, I had made friends with the other local kids. There weren't many other children my age, so perhaps it was inevitable that I would gravitate toward those who were. In Prineville, there were dozens of kids my age, but I didn't know any of them. I remember walking through the halls of the school between classes and being disoriented by the sheer number of people.

This feeling of alienation was exacerbated by the fact that some of the kids treated me cruelly, making fun of me because my clothes were out-of-date and not entirely clean. I sat in class listening to them, as they snickered and made verbal jabs at me. I had an Ocean Pacific-brand coat from Goodwill that, for some reason, they found particularly hilarious. I guess they saw it as out-of-date. They called me "OP" as a way of putting me down and drawing attention to it. Overall, going to school in Prineville was an unpleasant experience, one which I had to grit my teeth to get through.

LESSON: THE DIFFERENCE BETWEEN DREAMS AND VISIONS

When I talk about the distinction between visions and dreams, people sometimes get confused. They think I'm suggesting that they should know exactly where they're going to be thirty years from now. That's not how vision works. Life is unpredictable. It's not possible to plan exactly where we're going with certainty. What we *can* do is hold our desired outcomes in mind, move toward them, and be willing to adapt as circumstances alter.

One of my enduring frustrations in life is hearing teachers and authority figures exalt the power of dreaming. While they are aiming to inspire, I believe that they're leading people astray. It's easy to dream. What's hard is turning a dream into reality.

I know dozens of people who have grand dreams of what they wish to accomplish in life. Over the course of twenty to thirty years, however, I've seen too few of these dreams come to fruition, because the people in question have shown themselves unwilling to *work* for their success.

This is not to say that overnight success never happens. In my experience, however, overnight success is a consequence of years of work. It may take decades before results become apparent. Then, all of a sudden, everything falls into place, with great rewards. If you're putting one foot in front of the other, if you're consistently doing the work, it doesn't matter where you are now. You're moving in the right direction. If you're dreaming, but not doing, how will you get to where you want to go?

Imagine that you're climbing a tall tree. You can't see the top of the tree, but you keep taking the next step, moving a little further up the trunk. As you progress, you may only be able to see a few steps in front of you. Even if your visibility is hampered, however, you keep moving forward. Your final destination may be any one of the branches, even if you can't tell which one when you start. Keep moving upwards and the path will gradually become clearer. Sitting on the ground, dreaming about the end of each branch and imagining which one you want to reach, will get you nowhere. You need to take action.

Don't waste your precious time playing on your phone or watching television. I'm not saying that you need to cut these activities out of your life completely. Watching a movie with a partner, for example, can be an enjoyable way to build your relationship. I'm saying don't fill your life with these kinds of low-impact behaviors. Don't allow them to be the focus of your evenings and weekends. Don't turn them into habits. Focus on the activities that add value.

Remember, too, that distractions come in many forms. You may be going to work every day and engaging in seemingly productive activities. The question is whether those activities are taking you in the direction you want to go. Many of us become so caught up in the day-to-day treadmill of life that we forget to ask ourselves whether we're consistently doing work that moves us forward. Sometimes we may not see the fruits of our actions for a year, two years, or perhaps even five years. Yet, we know that we're laying the groundwork for future success. On many occasions in the business world, I have been hired to replace individuals who wore their workaholism as a badge of honor. They put in huge numbers of hours and ran around constantly as though their hair was on fire. Their approach, however, was ineffectual. Busyness does not equal productivity. If you want to become an agent of change, workaholism won't cut it.

This is why I encourage you to work persistently at your goals, rather than settling for dreams. I admire people who can craft a vision and *take steps* to move toward the fulfillment of that vision, not those with big dreams who never take action. There is a big distinction between a vision and a dream: a vision includes all the hard work that adds value and, ultimately, turns the dream into reality.

My mom's experiences in Paulina are a good example of the challenges of realizing a vision. She became fascinated by minerals and loved the idea of building a business to sell the minerals we gathered from the hills near the town. At the same time, she needed to focus on the day-to-day survival of her family, a task made that much harder by Pat's illness and incapacitation.

During this period of her life, my mom was beset by competing priorities. Her interest in mining, and the belief that she could find a way to make an acceptable living from that interest, was a driving force. She saw people who lived out in the woods, ran small-scale operations similar to the one she envisaged, and made a living. Not everyone would view the way those people lived as a success, but it appealed to my mom. It looked like a way she could develop a certain degree of financial stability without making too many compromises with the world.

At the same time, she knew she needed to work to afford mining tools and to feed me and my sisters. She had a vision of keeping the family together and ensuring that we were provided for, and that led her to go back to school and get a job.

No matter how tough things became, my mom continued to put one foot in front of the other. She did what she could to move toward a greater reality, while at the same time accepting that there were practical constraints on her ability to manifest her vision. Everything I knew of life told me that it was a constant struggle to get by, with little time for fun and games. Yet my mom was constantly working to give us a better future. She was a model of perseverance.

If you know that you want to move your life in a specific

direction—and I believe that's true of anyone who's growing—an element of challenge is indispensable. As soon as we accept our current situation, we fall into the trap of allowing life to live us, instead of living life. It's easy, safe, and comforting to fall into a routine and to live for the weekend. The next thing you know, you're a year older and you've accomplished nothing more than working during the week and hanging out on the couch on the weekend.

Remember why you're here on this planet and persevere toward the goals that you personally deem most important. You may not see results today, tomorrow, or even in a year. You may need to change direction at times to account for changing circumstances and priorities. But you can always persevere. You can always ask yourself what's most important right now and take a step in the right direction.

GOING BACK TO LA PINE

Midway through the winter, my mom came home and announced that she had quit nursing school and her job. She explained that, in her view, some of the treatment of the elderly people in the facility was unethical. She didn't feel comfortable working in that environment and felt that she could no longer be part of it. Between them, Pat and my mom decided that it was time to pull up stakes and return to the La Pine area.

We didn't go back to exactly the same place, however. We landed north of La Pine, close to a resort town named Sun River. In the summer, Sun River hosts golfers and mountain bikers. In the winter, it's a popular venue for skiers and snowboarders.

We parked our trailer in a little spot close to the Deschutes River, nestled between La Pine and Sun River, where we set up camp. We had minimal facilities and cooked our food on a small propane burner. It was winter when we arrived and the river was frozen over. Against the admonitions of my parents, I checked the thickness of the ice by sight and, deciding that it would support my weight, skated around the edges.

I was excited to be back in La Pine. When we lived in Paulina, the area was so secluded that I was largely isolated. There were hardly any other kids my age. At school in Prineville, meanwhile, I was subject to a lot of ridicule, which made me glad to leave. La Pine felt much more open and friendly.

My mom picked up a job as a housekeeper in Sun River, cleaning resorts, condos, and other holiday homes. For the second time, I enrolled in La Pine Middle School. Aside from traveling to visit my father and returning to Sue and Tom's Mountain to see Ganya, moving back to La Pine was the first time I had left a place, then come back. In a childhood filled with new and unaccustomed experiences, I was looking forward to seeing familiar faces and places.

INTERLUDE #2

PROACTIVITY

1989–1992 (AGE TWELVE TO FIFTEEN), LA PINE, OREGON

I sat at what passed for our dining room table, although it was closer in size to a fold-out card table. A candle burned on the table and a wood stove smoldered in the background, warming the house and simultaneously heating a small pot of water. Using a wood-burning stove dries out the air, so we always kept a pot of water simmering to counteract that tendency and add some humidity to the air. It was a useful resource, too, for a family who didn't have easy access to hot water. My mom also used it for hot drinks.

On the table was a roll of silver wire and a collection of porcupine quills, claws, and teeth. I had brought these treasures with me to La Pine and I was making them into a necklace. My first task was to clip off the tip of the quill, the part that enters the skin. Porcupine quills are heavily barbed. Once they enter the flesh, they're extremely difficult to remove. My second task was to clip off the other end, where the quill grew out of the porcupine's body. This too was pointed, albeit not as dangerous as the quill tip.

I threaded the teeth, claws, and quills onto the silver wire. I placed one tooth at the center of the necklace, then two quills on either side. I then added a layer of claws, followed by another layer of quills, continuing until the necklace was complete. I used a pair of needle-nose pliers to wrap the ends of the wire around each other and attach a small clamp to hold the ends together. When the necklace was finished, it was reminiscent of Native American jewelry. I made several of these necklaces and wore them to school. I liked them because they were unique, my own creation. I even sold some to classmates.

THEME: A BURGEONING SENSE OF PROACTIVITY

Over the course of this short chapter, you'll see how I began to take control of my life. Although I was still fairly young, I felt a strong sense that it was time to take on as much responsibility as I could, shaping my environment and having a positive impact on my family.

In my adult life, this **proactivity** has played an essential role in my achievements. Without the capacity to assess a situation, recognize how it could be improved, and take action to make it better, I could never have attained the success I have.

The stories in this chapter represent the first stirrings of that active approach to life. I engaged seriously with school, took an interest in my athletic development, and took the first steps down my entrepreneurial path. I was determined to be the driver of my own life and I never wanted to feel as though I was merely along for the ride. Whatever happened, I chose to take ownership of my own development.

FROM CABIN TO CABIN

Our first winter and spring back in the La Pine area we continued to live in our trailer and in tents, moving from one campsite to another. The US Forest Service in that part of the state was highly active, due to the numbers of fish and wildlife they have a responsibility to protect, so camping was only permitted for up to two weeks at a time. We stayed in each campsite until we saw a forest service ranger, who inevitably asked us whether we were camping or living. We would tell the ranger we were camping, at which point we had two weeks to stay until we were forced to move on.

Often the location of our campsite was out of range of the bus service, so one of my parents drove me to the nearest bus stop, then picked me up after school. Sometimes, however, they went out fishing or drinking and forgot to collect me from the bus stop. I would hang out for an hour and, if nobody showed, I'd walk the couple of miles home from the bus stop. On one occasion, the bus driver asked me about my situation and drove me all the way to the beginning of the dirt road leading to the campsite where we were living. That left me with only a half-mile hike.

Toward the start of summer, we moved into a tiny fifteen feet by fifteen feet cabin. Although our landlord owned several cabins, only one was initially available. It was an upgrade from the trailer, but still an extremely small space for six people. It, too, had no running water or electricity. I think it was an old hunting cabin, where people came to hang out while they fished or hunted, so there wasn't much need for amenities.

Over the course of the year, as new accommodations became available, we moved to progressively larger cabins. The second was a little bigger and offered electricity, but no hot water. Just like in Paulina, I bathed by heating up a pot of water and pouring it over my head. I only did this about once a week and, by this time, I was entering my teenage years, so I was more vulnerable to body odor. In Prineville, the kids were standoffish, even cruel. La Pine, by contrast, was a friendlier environment. Even so, I was still harassed at school on occasion for not washing more frequently.

I reconnected with friends I'd left behind when I moved away in fifth grade. This was also when I discovered that the friend who had done my writing for me when I broke my arm had died in a car accident while I was in Paulina. Other kids asked me whether I remembered him, but I couldn't picture his face. This was at a time when I was old enough to generate vivid memories—I have a clear recollection of breaking my arm—yet I have completely forgotten someone who did all my coursework for much of fifth grade.

My school grades were consistently good during this time. I received As in almost every class. In Paulina, I had already done all the work we were supposed to do in seventh grade, so I was bored most of the time.

We ended up moving again, this time into a cabin that was large enough for me to have my own bedroom—even though it was so cramped there was barely room for a bed. My sisters shared another bedroom. The bedrooms where my sisters and I slept were extensions of the original structure. The main cabin consisted of a living space and a kitchen, with the bedrooms housed under a secondary roof. Even this third cabin was too small for the entire family, so my parents lived in the trailer. Although this cabin had electricity, running water, and a wood stove and was definitely an improvement, it was still quite basic. The interior was unfinished, with raw insulation visible.

It was here that I began to make necklaces out of porcupine quills. It was also where I started my own landscaping business.

One of several cabins where we lived in La Pine. Few had electricity or running water.

WORKING, LIFTING, MAKING

The owners of the cabins introduced me to several older couples who wanted help taking care of their lawns. Soon, I was booked solid all weekend long, riding my ten-speed bike from house to house and mowing lawns. I didn't have my own mowing equipment, but all the couples I worked for did. There were many retirees in the La Pine area, and they were more than happy to pay me to take the work of maintaining their gardens off their hands.

I loved riding my bike and often went out on long rides—as long as twenty miles—for the sheer pleasure of exploring different areas of the town. I also began to train and lift weights during this time. At first, my only access to weights was at high school. Soon, however, I found a pair of ankle weights at Goodwill and supplemented my training by strapping them to my ankles and going out for runs. I also did jump squats until I was exhausted and did hundreds of push-ups. I had no real idea what I was doing. I simply picked up a few basic moves and repeated them until my muscles were so fatigued that, over the following days, I could hardly move.

Flexing during a visit to my father in Sonoma, California. I was about sixteen years old and getting more serious about weight training.

Turning natural materials into art had become some-thing of a theme in my family by this time, and we had a burgeoning collection of art pieces made of rocks and other things we found in the woods. Pat loved carving, particularly when he could get hold of tree burls. A burl is a section of tree that has grown in on itself, forming a big, solid knot. Burls polish up well and make interesting art, because the grain of the wood forms intriguing patterns. I went for long hikes in the woods seeking out burls. When I found good ones, I broke or cut them out of the trees they were in and brought them back for Pat to carve.

Those first months back in La Pine, I spent most of my time making necklaces, foraging for burls, and managing my fledgling landscaping business. When I wasn't doing those, I trained until I dropped or went on long bike rides around the local area. Although this was a relatively settled time in my life, with few major episodes, there were occasional moments of drama.

IT'S RAINING ANTS

On one occasion, following a protracted rainstorm, I was sitting in our cabin and I heard a sound like a thousand raindrops hitting the ceiling. "Why does it still sound as though it's raining?" I said. I walked outside to check that the rain had ended. It had. Then I walked around the house in search of the source of the noise. It sounded as though it was coming from above my sisters' bunk bed.

I called Pat and my mom and explained what I could hear, and we all went into the bedroom to explore further. The cabin didn't have a proper ceiling, only raw insulation, so I peeled back the edge of the insulation to investigate.

Suddenly, millions upon millions of ants rained into the room. Imagine tipping a five-gallon bucket, full to the brim with ants, into your bedroom. The floor was thick with them.

Naturally, my sisters were freaked out by the massive numbers of ants pouring into their room. As we pulled back the edge of the insulation, they were sitting on their bunk bed, so they had a front row seat for a scene that looked like something out of an extreme nature documentary. Even today, they still laughingly recount the event.

Clearly, the ants had chosen our roof as a nice warm space to live during the rains. There were so many of them that, as they moved around inside the roof cavity, they made a sound like rain. It took a long while to make sure that we had removed them. We even pulled out all the insulation from the roof. Afterward, we couldn't afford to replace the insulation, and the landlord lacked either the money or the motivation—or both—so it remained bare, uncovered plywood for the rest of our stay.

A SENSE OF BELONGING

For perhaps the first time in my life, I felt part of a consistent group of friends during this second stint in La Pine. When I returned, I reconnected with a few people

I had known the first time I lived in the area, but at that age, a couple of years felt like a long time. People had begun to move on and develop new friendship networks. As I started at a new school once again, I didn't have any friends who I hung out with on a consistent basis.

With no one to shoot the breeze with during the gaps between classes, I used to go directly from one lesson to the next. I picked up my books, walked to the location of my next class, and simply sat there, waiting until class started.

One day, while I sat alone at lunchtime, a tall, red-haired kid named Greg approached me.

"Hey, come sit with us."

"Okay, that sounds good," I said without hesitation.

I walked over to a table where Greg introduced me to a couple of other guys named Matt and Curt. They were a group of oddballs. Greg used to hang with the stoner crowd, smoking weed and listening to heavy metal. Curt was a Jehovah's Witness, and Matt was a nerd who loved reading and video games. I soon discovered that Greg had made a conscious decision to break away from the stoner group and pull together a new crew. He felt that he was at risk of making some poor life choices and he wanted to change direction.

"We're friends now," he told me.

"All right," I said. "Sounds good."

And we were. We rolled together the rest of the time I lived in La Pine.

When eighth grade started, Greg suggested that we started doing track together. His older brother was a track and field star. I liked being friends with him, so I was willing to go along with his suggestion to sign up for track and field. This was when I discovered that, for low-income families, the school waived the costs of getting involved in sports.

Although I was smart and nerdy, I already had a distinct interest in physical activity. Getting involved in track and field cemented this interest and started me down the path toward further involvement in sports.

Running track and field as a freshman in high school. During this period, my interest in sports and physical development really took off.

LESSON: EXERCISING PROACTIVITY

It's incredibly easy to attribute your situation in life to external circumstances. This is particularly true if you're in a negative environment. Perhaps you've lost your job or you're struggling in some other fashion.

It's true that you can't control everything in your life, but you can take ownership of *elements* of your reality and take action. At times, the changes you can make may be small. You may find yourself thinking that it'll be ten years before you work yourself into a better situation. Even if that's the case, don't succumb to despair. Start doing what you can to improve your life. Who knows what will happen in the future. Maybe you'll carve out an unexpected opportunity for yourself a couple of years down the line. As much as you can, take control of your life.

I attribute a lot of my current success to the habit of proactivity I started developing in seventh grade. I earned money from my landscaping business, for example, which also enabled me to contribute to the family household budget. I took an interest in sports, which gradually led to some outstanding athletic achievements. Even prior to this period, I proactively studied every page of every textbook in the two-room schoolhouse in Paulina, meaning that by the time I got to La Pine I was mostly repeating material I already understood. That made school easy for me and meant I had more energy to dedicate to other pursuits.

In the following chapters, you'll begin to see where proactivity led me. I didn't know exactly where I was going, but I knew I could develop the habit of moving the needle a little bit. If you're not sure how to move forward, recognize that proactivity is a form of preparation. It prepares you for a better future. Yes, you'll need to have an idea of where you're going. Nonetheless, remember that not everything will turn out the way you anticipate. Even if you encounter setbacks and things aren't working out as you hoped, retain your motivation and keep doing the work.

A SETTLED HOME

Years before we moved back to La Pine, Pat put in a disability claim relating to his broken arm. It seemed that nothing would ever come of it, which is why he continued to work for so long with a broken arm. Eventually, however, he won his disability case, receiving a small amount of back pay. He had an operation to fix his arm, and he and my mom made a down payment on a double-wide mobile home.

Pat's surgery felt like a big deal. The capacity to purchase our own home felt like an even bigger deal. In Paulina, we had tried to buy the cabin where we had lived for a time, but even in an area where property prices were rock bottom, we couldn't afford it. In La Pine, we finally had the money to settle somewhere of our own.

Admittedly, the money came from a court case rather than directly from labor, which might initially seem to go against my parents' values. On this occasion, however, they felt that the windfall was deserved, due to all the hard, physical work Pat had done over the years with a broken arm. My parents were excited, and they transmitted their excitement to the rest of us.

It wasn't a luxurious place to live, but it was secure. When we moved in, the whole yard was strewn with trash, along with the rusted-out chassis of a Ford Courier with no engine. We filled the entire truck with the debris from the yard, almost burying it.

Despite these limitations, I loved this new home. We hung old sheets in the windows and built a countertop so that we had somewhere to install a sink. For perhaps the first time in my life, I knew that I had a safe, stable home base to serve as a foundation. I saw it as a platform for future success in business and training. While we bounced around from place to place, it was challenging to sustain my fledgling business and my training regime. The trailer felt like a stepping stone from which I could leap to greater heights.

CHAPTER FIVE

DISCOVERY

1992–1995 (AGE FIFTEEN TO EIGHTEEN), LA PINE, OREGON

After sports, in the evenings, I did shift work in Sun River. I hitched a ride with friends and put in a shift as a busboy or a dishwasher. One particular evening, I was sitting downstairs in the break room hammering out an essay for the local newspaper, the *Bend Bulletin*.

I had applied for several scholarships at Oregon State, the largest engineering school in Oregon, none of which were awarded to me. In an effort to raise money to go to college, I started applying for smaller, local scholarships. Unfortunately, these were too small to make a major contribution to college costs. I was becoming frustrated.

I knew my parents didn't have the financial resources to

support me through college, so I was beginning to wonder whether I would be able to go at all. I was contemplating finding a place in Sun River and continuing to work.

These thoughts were rolling around my head as I composed my essay, an entry into a competition run by the *Bend Bulletin* with the prize of—you guessed it—a scholarship. I wrote about my childhood experiences, how hard I'd worked to get to where I already was, and how frustrated I was that I couldn't see a way to fund my further studies.

The tone of my writing was very emotional. The first two paragraphs read:

> "A family of six lives in a sixteen-foot trailer by a mountain stream. The oldest of their children sleeps in the back of their truck through a 20-below winter. Both parents are unemployed, the father disabled.
>
> They move from town to town looking for housing that is affordable, while the mother works at odd jobs. Sometimes during the summer they set up tents and pretend that they're just on a camping trip. A camping trip that lasts for years. This family is my family."

I submitted the essay and, a few weeks later, I received a call from the *Bend Bulletin*. They called me while I was at school, because they didn't know how else to get a hold of me. I walked into the office, picked up the phone, and the guy on the other end of the line told me he had some bad news for me. He told me I hadn't won the scholarship. It was awarded to a kid from Bend who was a valedictorian and was going to MIT, and barely beat me out. In lieu of a scholarship, on the other hand, the *Bend Bulletin* wanted to run an article about me.

At the time, I didn't go to school in the mornings. Instead of studying in my morning block, I got credit for the job I did in the evenings, because I was supporting my family. Some people advised me that, if I wanted to go to college, working a job wasn't a great move. They suggested that I take as many advanced placement classes as I could, which I did, but I balanced that with working and bringing in income. That decision probably played a role in causing me to miss out on the scholarship. The kid who got it had a better academic record. He was going to a bigger school. By the numbers, he looked more qualified than me. Fortunately for me, someone at the newspaper wanted to help me out by telling my story.

I agreed and the newspaper sent a writer and a photographer to take some pictures of me. The shots show me standing with my parents in front of the mobile home where we lived. The *Bend Bulletin* published a piece based on my essay on the front page, and the story was picked up by all the major cities in the Northwest. It ran in the *Seattle Times* and the *Eugene Register-Guard*, and I think also in Portland. Following its publication, I was pulled out of class several times to be interviewed on the radio. Soon after, donations began to roll in. My high school wrestling coach, Rusty Zysett, set up a trust fund that enabled me to buy a computer and, later, some supplies for college.

Then, I received a call from the Oregon Institute of Technology (OIT), in southern Oregon, a highly technical college with a strong engineering focus. I had been set on studying at Oregon State, so I hadn't considered OIT, let alone applied. When they called, however, I agreed to visit the college. My math teacher stepped in and drove me and my parents down to southern Oregon, because we didn't have a vehicle capable of making the trip at the time.

I checked out the college, spent some time with some of the teachers and administration staff, and they offered me a full-ride scholarship. They pulled together a number of grants and scholarships, factored in my financial aid, and put together a package that covered all my expenses. I accepted their offer. My parents were delighted that I was going to college. I've mentioned previously that they had strong feelings about charity, which they saw as stemming from pity. This was different. I had worked extremely hard to secure opportunities, and they felt I had earned the advantages I received.

I had imagined that most people at school were aware of my living conditions, but apparently that wasn't the case. When my story was featured in the newspaper, it was an eye-opening experience for a lot of people. Friends from school suddenly looked at me differently. People from all corners of the state walked into the restaurant where I was waiting tables and said, "Hey, are you that kid from the newspaper?"

The exposure I received from the article in the *Bend Bulletin* was my first experience of being in the public eye. I went from feeling isolated and struggling to get to college, to suddenly having a scholarship at OIT.

Things were moving quickly and everything felt a little surreal.

Hard work, straight-A's and frustration

LaPine scholar longs for college

"A family of six lives in a 16 foot trailer by a mountain stream. The oldest of the children sleeps in the back of their truck through a 20 below winter. Both parents are unemployed, the father disabled.

"They move from town to town looking for housing that is affordable, while the mother works at odd jobs. Sometimes during the summer they set up tents and pretend that they're just on a camping trip. A camping trip that lasts for years. This family is my family..."

—Chris Duffin, 1995 essay

By Jeff Nielson
Bulletin Staff Writer

LaPINE — Chris Duffin will graduate from LaPine High School in June with a straight-A average. His letterman's jacket is covered with athletic and academic medals.

His teachers and peers say the quiet, stocky 18-year-old is a leader by example — one who volunteers to help build houses for Habitat for Humanity and distribute Christmas baskets to the needy. They can't understand how he can compile such an outstanding record, yet not win a scholarship from Oregon State University to help cover the $10,000-a-year cost.

And there is no other way Chris can afford tuition, fees, books and living expenses. He and his family have been homeless and hungry, and are still struggling with poverty.

His stepfather, Pat Smith, is

Chris Duffin has suffered setbacks, but that hasn't kept him from achieving academic and athletic excellence

Schools lack aid money

"They told us as long as the kids were clean and fed, they were okay," Cindy Smith recalled.

record and finished second in the 172-pound weight class at the 3A state championships.

Bulletin/Dean Guernsey

The cover story written about me in the Bend Bulletin in 1995, just before I graduated.

THEME: A PERIOD OF SELF-DISCOVERY

I knew what I wanted to do, but I didn't know how to make it happen. Everything I did, from choosing and applying to a school, to navigating financial aid, I did myself.

When I reflect back on this period of my life, I'm still something of a mystery to myself. I came from a family where no one went to college and had little mentorship. My parents wanted me to go to college, but couldn't provide me with much in the way of guidance or support. Admittedly, I was in advanced classes, rubbing shoulders with people for whom college seemed like a normal, natural progression. As one of their classmates, I felt this expectation. I picked up the message that everyone should go to college, and I decided that's what I would do, too. Nonetheless, it's hard for me to understand how I formed such a strong determination.

For all my parents' good qualities, they were totally unfamiliar with the world of education. They simply lacked the expertise to support me along the path I chose. My parents weren't familiar with the system, so they didn't know how to help. I was also unaware of anyone at school whose job it was to support students gearing for college. Most other students seemed to rely on their parents to push them in the right direction.

To me, however, the process was completely alien. I knew

that I needed to fill in my student aid paperwork, which involved collecting some information from my parents. I had a vague idea of where I wanted to go, too. I wanted to go to Oregon State because it was the biggest wrestling school in the Northwest. By this time—as you'll read about later in this chapter—I was wrestling regularly. Oregon State was home to a collegiate national champion in my weight class, and I wanted to go there so I could train with him. What I lacked was a practical understanding of how to get there.

Yet, instead, I found my way to a full-ride scholarship at OIT. Moreover, this period of my life ended up playing an essential role in building the structures that I later used to support myself. It was a time of **discovery**, reflected in the stories that make up this chapter. By putting one foot in front of another, I tapped into resources—both internal and external—I hadn't known were available. Without the shifts that occurred during this time, would I have pulled myself out of the environment in which I grew up? I don't know for sure. What I can say is that my experiences during these years set me on a new path, which ultimately led me to where I am today.

A yearbook photo of me from an advanced placement math class, during my senior year in high school. I had just finished a workout and was sporting a stringer tank. I thought I looked great.

STABILITY AT LAST

Compared with some of the places my family had lived previously, our new mobile home felt like a palace. It was the first time we had a stable place to live and knew we wouldn't need to move away at the drop of a hat.

When I say, "new home," however, you might think it was more luxurious than it was. It was a double-wide mobile home with an extension—containing additional rooms—built off the back. The extension sat directly on the ground, so it was certainly not up to code.

Inside the mobile home there were no doors. To compensate for this, we hung sheets across all the doorways. Our bedrooms and the bathroom were only separated from the rest of the house by sheets. There was no kitchen, so we rigged up a makeshift plywood countertop using some old two-by-fours and a used sink. Pots, pans, plates, and cutlery we stacked on boxes underneath the sink.

La Pine is hot in the summer and cold in the winter, and our home did little to shelter us from the heat or protect us from the cold. There was no double glazing, just single-pane windows that cranked open or shut. When the wind blew, it came straight through the window. To insulate ourselves from the worst of the cold, we put together our own insulation by taping and stapling a sheet of plastic over the inside and outside of the windows.

The mobile home may not have been fancy, but it did have hot running water and electricity. To us, that made it seem comfortable.

MY HIGH SCHOOL WRESTLING CAREER

It was while we lived in this mobile home that I started lifting weights seriously. Previously, I had focused mainly on jump squats and push-ups. Sometimes I trained at high school, but I wanted a place to work out outside of high school hours. I scoured the nickel ads and found cheap pieces of exercise equipment—plates, benches, and dumbbells—and used them to build my own home gym on the back porch. When winter came, and it got too cold to work out outside, I moved my equipment inside to my bedroom.

I started wrestling my freshman year. I was already doing track and field, which was a spring sport, and my mom didn't want me to play football, so I took up wrestling instead. I knew I was strong for my weight and—through lifting—I was already developing a lot of confidence and self-esteem in my physicality.

My first year on the wrestling team was an eye-opening experience. Wrestling is a sport that a lot of people start young, at the age of five, six, or seven. As a freshman, I was competing against guys who had been wrestling almost their entire lives, and who knew moves I'd never encountered. That first year was a bit of a grind. I lost my first twenty-five matches in a row.

The wrestling team at my high school was strong and the coach pushed the athletes hard. A lot of people dropped out during the year. I didn't drop out, but I did get a reputation as a "fish." In wrestling terminology, a fish is a guy that flops around—like a fish out of water—and is easy to beat.

Then, right at the end of the season, I won two matches. Laid out like that, it might sound like a horrible experience, but I enjoyed it. I liked the way the sport challenged me, and I appreciated the demands it made on my body. At first, I wasn't very good. However, I could see the benefits of the work I put in, and that inspired me to continue.

My freshman year, I cut weight to stay under 141 pounds and compete in a lighter weight class. I thought that would make my bouts easier. By sophomore year, however, I gave up on that strategy. Instead, I trained hard in my home gym, bulked up, and competed at 168 pounds. It was a big jump.

During my sophomore year, I won twenty-five matches in a row, losing only two. It was a record that qualified me for districts.

I was a nerdy kid, so the physical nature of wrestling acted as a natural counterbalance to that tendency. I also liked the accountability that came with wrestling. If I lost, it was because I hadn't wrestled well enough. If I won, it was because I had done well. There was no one else to blame. It could be a grueling sport, especially for those who chose to push themselves hard. I loved to push myself, in an effort to explore my boundaries and reach the outer limits of my capabilities. During my sophomore, junior, and senior years, I signed on to run cross-country in the spring, purely so I could stay in shape ready for the return of wrestling season.

I was probably the largest cross-country runner in the

state, and definitely one of the slowest. I didn't care about that, though. I was only interested in the impact on my wrestling performance. My old cross-country coach likes to tell the story of a school trip that involved both the high school's cross-country team and the football team. We had a meet at the same place the football team played a game, and the football players were complaining about riding with the cross-country team, who they branded "lame" and "losers." My coach told the football players to say that to the next person who boarded the bus. Sure enough, I walked up the stairs and the entire bus fell silent.

During my sophomore year, following my 25-2 record in the regular season, I was knocked out in districts. The same thing happened my junior year. By senior year, however, I felt strong and ready. I sought out competition wherever I could find it, jumping up weight classes to wrestle state champions at different weights. At this point, I was co-captain of the wrestling team, with a heavyweight named Sean Tinker. Sean weighed about 275 pounds, and he was my main sparring partner. He was the only person on our team who still presented me with a challenge due to his massive weight advantage over me. In addition to Sean, I sometimes sparred with the school's assistant coach, who was an adult with many years of experience.

Despite this progress, I had already lost to three different people in the district over the course of the year. My weight class in districts was stacked with talent and—with only the top two performers making it through—it looked as though I would struggle to qualify for state. A couple of weeks prior to our districts meet, my coach approached me and asked what I thought would happen. I looked at him and said, matter-of-factly, "I'm going to win and go on to state." Based on my record over the year, that prediction seemed unlikely to come true. Even today, I'm not sure why I felt such certainty about the outcome. When I told my coach I would win, however, I felt no doubt at all. I was going to win districts.

I wasn't a particularly technical wrestler. Some of my team members and opponents knew dozens of moves. I had precisely three. I knew how to take down. I knew how to escape a hold. And I knew how to block a shot. My thinking was that if I knew how to block a shot and escape from holds, I couldn't be taken down. Therefore, I couldn't lose. I became incredibly good at these three moves and ignored all other techniques since it was a style that served me well.

My coach liked to use me as an example. He told other members of the team that I had the worst shot in the squad, but I always got it. When I grabbed an opponent, I might take hold of their leg with just two fingers. Then, I'd pull until I got it by three fingers. After a bit more work,

I'd have it by four fingers, then my whole hand. At which point, I'd pull my opponent in and take him down. Some of my wrestling was ugly, but I knew my strengths and refused to be beaten.

When I reached districts, one of the people who'd beaten me earlier in the year was knocked out by someone else, so I only faced rematches against two of the three. I made it through every match at districts without conceding a single offensive point, an extremely rare occurrence. This means that no one succeeded in taking me down or making a shot against me. The only time my opponents scored points was when they escaped from a hold, registering a defensive point. This usually happened when I let them go so I could take them down again. In the final, I met one of the guys who had beaten me during the season. I won resoundingly, again without conceding a single offensive point.

I became that year's district champion.

Winning the district title in my senior year, without conceding a single offensive point. My coach is handing me the award.

The next challenge was state. Three of us made it from my high school: Sean Tinker, myself, and one other kid. The state championships were held in a big auditorium with 360-degree seating around the mats. There were television cameras recording the event and broadcasting news of the championships on local stations. It felt like a freakily strange environment to me.

State championships run for several days. I started winning my matches and, the next thing I knew, I was in the state finals, again without conceding a single offensive point. My opponent, named Baumgartner, had won the Oregon state championships for the previous three years. Meanwhile, I was an unknown who had never previously made it past districts, with a wrestling style composed of three moves. Prior to the match, one of my coaches came up to me and told me that he'd heard some spectators asking, "Is Baumgartner going to pin him in the first round or the second round? That's the question."

I'm not sure why my coach told me this. Perhaps he thought it would fire me up. Unfortunately, it was counterproductive. As an athlete, I'm highly cerebral. I figure out what works, and I execute it. When I heard my chances being dismissed, I got quite emotional and stepped out onto the mat feeling as though I had something to prove.

In the first round, I realized that I was the superior wrestler. I could position my opponent wherever I wanted. I could take him down. I could prevent him from taking me down. Just as with every other bout through districts and state, there was no way he could beat me.

In wrestling, there are three rounds. In the first round, both wrestlers start in a neutral standing position. In the second round, there's a coin toss. Whoever wins gets to choose whether to start in the up position (in control) or the down position (needing to escape). The person in the down position has their lower leg on the ground, their hands on the floor in front of them, and their butt resting on their heels. The one in the up position places one leg beside their opponent, with an arm wrapped around their opponent's midriff, touching their navel, and the other arm resting on their elbow. Smart wrestlers always defer, allowing their opponent to choose which position to start in for the second round and retaining their choice for the decisive, final round.

Throughout my entire high school wrestling career, whenever I won the toss, I chose to defer. In the state final, however, I departed from that plan. I didn't even know who had been talking trash about me, but I was determined to prove them wrong. I chose to start in the down position, with the intention of standing up, escaping, turning around, taking Baumgartner down, and winning the bout emphatically. I knew how to do three things: takedowns, escapes, and blocks. None of those moves involve turning someone over and pinning them. It's almost impossible to do that to a good wrestler, so I never even tried. I won my matches in three rounds, on points.

A little stubborn and a little overconfident, I chose the state final to do something different. I was too cocky to get into my escape position fast enough, and Baumgartner jumped on me and executed a move called a leg ride. Leg rides are usually the prerogative of lighter wrestlers. Competing in the 174-pound weight class, I hadn't spent a lot of time working on escaping a leg ride. I never needed to. Baumgartner turned me over, pinned me, and won the match. I walked away devastated, because I knew I was the better wrestler and I lost due to my own choices.

Besting an opponent in the wrestling ring. This was in my senior year, before I went on to win the district finals in the 174-pound class.

Nonetheless, when I reflected on my experience, I found much cause for satisfaction. From a complete novice a few years earlier, I worked my way all the way through districts to the final match in the state championships. I was only defeated by a guy who had already been state champion for the previous three years. And even then, I knew I was better than him.

BETTER LIVING THROUGH PAINTBALL

In my junior and senior year, as my friends began to drive, we purchased some used paintball guns. We used some of our income from work to purchase basic paintball gear and we began to play. Most of us worked in service industries, so we were on a swing shift. That meant we had our

Saturdays free to play, before heading over to Sun River to work.

Sometimes we found old, abandoned houses or rock caverns to use as paintball sites. With so much national forest land and in central Oregon, we were spoiled for choice. It was an activity that bonded my high school group of friends together for some years, even after we left La Pine for college.

After about a year of weekend paintballing, we were fairly good. We started to play competitively, traveling around the state and entering tournaments. For me, it was a fun outlet for my energy and an enjoyable way to be a teenager—a part of my personality I hadn't had a great deal of opportunity to indulge. Of course, it was also a great way to get away from my home environment.

I liked to tinker with the guns. I took them apart and modified them. For example, I found ways of improving them so that they performed better in cold-weather conditions. I polished the triggers to improve trigger response and adapted the valves so that air flowed through them more quickly, increasing the range of the guns. Paintball would be a part of my life for the next several years, bonding me to my friends and giving me an escape from the challenges of daily life.

A UNIQUE THANKSGIVING DINNER

Despite our stable home—Pat's disability checks, my mom's job, and the income I brought in from working—we never seemed to have enough money. Putting food on the table felt like a constant struggle.

One year, a couple of months prior to Thanksgiving, Pat spotted an ad offering free rabbits to a good home. Pat and I jumped in the truck and picked up three rabbits, one for each of my sisters. We built a makeshift cage for them in the yard and Pat named them Breakfast, Lunch, and Dinner. I had no idea how prophetic those names would prove.

I'll never know whether Pat always intended to make the rabbits live up to their names, or whether it was mere coincidence. He always had quite a dark sense of humor and it's possible he was attempting to impart some kind of life lesson. It's equally possible we ran out of money over Thanksgiving and his eyes lit upon the nearest source of fresh meat. In my eyes, they were always our pets, until suddenly they weren't.

On Thanksgiving morning, Pat announced that we didn't have money for turkey and enlisted my help in killing Breakfast, Lunch, and Dinner. We grabbed one of them at a time, held them between our legs, and twisted their necks until they broke. Then we gutted them, skinned them, and brought them inside, where my mom cooked them. We ate them with instant mashed potatoes and iceberg lettuce.

Naturally, my sisters were devastated when they discovered that their prized pets became our Thanksgiving meal. They bawled all day and, when we sat down to dinner, they still had streaks of tears running down their faces. Somehow, however, they managed to find some humor in the situation. My littlest sister, eating the rabbit that had been known as Dinner, looked up at one point and said, "Mmm, Dinner tastes so good."

LIFE AT HOME BEGINS TO DETERIORATE

With no classes in my morning block, I often worked as a busboy or a dishwasher late into the night. When I awoke early in the morning, it was common to see Pat or my mom digging through my pants in the half-light, pulling out cash so that they could purchase food, supplies, or beer from the local store. They always framed this as borrowing money, although I never saw most of that money again.

I wrote off what they took and accepted it as my contribution to the household. Over time, however, my parents began to drink more and more. At this point in his life, Pat was quite incapacitated. With a broken arm and weakened lungs, he couldn't work, and winning his disability settlement meant that he no longer needed to. Perhaps unsure what else to do with himself, he spent most of his time sitting around the house, watching television, and drinking.

When Pat sat in front of the television and drank, he became obsessed with the news. The news was his world. While this was happening, O.J. Simpson went on trial for the murders of Nicole Brown Simpson and Ron Goldman. Pat watched the whole trial, all day, every day. When my mom arrived home from work, he started talking to her about developments in the trial.

It was a long trial and, after several months, my mom flipped. She got home, Pat started telling her about the O.J. Simpson trial, and she yelled, "I don't want to hear it. Don't tell me another fucking word about the O.J. Simpson trial. I don't want to hear about it anymore." The following day, she arrived home and he jumped up, ran over to her, and started telling her about the latest developments in the O.J. Simpson trial. She was at the fridge door, getting something out of the fridge, and she said, "I told you I don't want to hear it." Then she swung the fridge door at him, hitting him full in the face. He was knocked out cold and lost two front teeth, which he replaced with fake teeth. After that, he never said another word about the O.J. Simpson trial.

My mom, meanwhile, began getting into scrapes caused by alcohol consumption. In Oregon, there's a single highway that connects Bend, La Pine, and numerous other towns and cities, all the way down to Klamath Falls, where my future college was located. At one stage, this highway connects to I-97 via a T-junction. As an interstate highway, I-97 is a busy road, at least two and, in some places, four lanes wide. My mom got drunk one night and drove through the intersection at full speed, somehow missing the traffic barreling along I-97, and launching the car into the forest on the other side of the highway. To avoid getting a DUI, she ran away before the police arrived. She was lucky to escape with her life.

On another occasion, she climbed a barbed wire fence as she ran away from another drunken incident. As she scaled the fence, she sliced her arm open on one of the barbs and passed out, probably from the pain. When she woke up she was still hanging from the fence, cut nearly to the bone and bleeding heavily. Fortunately, she managed to get to a hospital and get herself patched up before the situation got any worse.

Alcohol also fueled fights between Pat and my mom. She often retreated to the trailer or lost herself working on her rocks, as a way to avoid interacting with him. After we settled in La Pine, they had managed to accumulate equipment to work the minerals we had collected in Paulina, so we had a selection of rock saws, buffing wheels, and sanders—enough to turn the rocks into attractive pieces of jewelry. I helped to keep the rock saw supplied with cutting stones. Pat occasionally made some jewelry. My mom, however, did most of the work.

As a consequence of my parents' drinking, conditions at home deteriorated quite severely. I think the fact that we were settled in one place for such a relatively long time also played a part. Pat was drunk most of the time and never did any cleaning. My mom worked in the daytime, but when she returned home, she had little appetite for interacting with Pat or spending time in the house. Instead, she hid in the trailer and she, too, was soon drunk.

The house filled up with garbage, toys, and other detritus. There were trails of discarded waste throughout the building. Both my parents also smoked incessantly, creating a perpetual smoke haze throughout the house.

GRADUATING, WITHOUT MY PARENTS

The day of graduation, I was over at my friend Greg's house playing some games. Greg lived about fifteen minutes from high school and we realized that we needed to hurry if we were going to make it in time. We picked up our gowns and I picked up a notepad. I was valedictorian, so it was my responsibility to give a speech at graduation. Like most teenagers, I had a habit of procrastinating until the last minute; I wrote my speech in the car on the fifteen-minute journey into school. Looking back, it would have made more sense to write the speech in advance and practice it several times in advance. As with most elements of high school, however, I was used to coming through at the last moment, so that's what I did with my speech.

We arrived at graduation and I gave my speech. We posed for photos and I received some awards, such as best student athlete—incidentally, the same award my mom won when she was in high school. At the time, I didn't notice my parents' absence. It was only years later that I discovered they had shown up drunk. My wrestling coach, whose job it was to usher parents into the graduation hall, turned them away, telling them that he didn't want me to remember my graduation in that fashion. It seemed sad and appropriate that, for all they had done for me, they didn't watch me graduate.

LESSON: DISCOVERING YOUR STRENGTH

There are many ways we typically assess our success in life. Perhaps you judge yourself on the size of your house, the quality of your job, or how much money you earn. There's no objective way to measure success, however. We all have our own strengths and we all need to find the arenas in which we can excel.

If this sounds like a cliché, that's because it's true. You will never know where your strengths lie until you begin to challenge yourself, step out of your comfort zone, and explore your capabilities. The idea of being a tryhard is often treated with disdain. I think that's a mistake. Until you expend effort, how do you know what you're good at? You can only discover your own greatness through trial and error.

When I lived in a cabin in La Pine, there were numerous other families in similar situations. Many of those families contained kids approximately my age. As far as I'm aware, I'm the only one who made the decision to go to college. Most lived under the assumption that the horizons they knew dictated their choices and opportunities in life. Of course, that became a self-fulfilling prophecy. They led the lives they expected to lead.

The only reason I made it out of that environment was my willingness to explore my potential and discover what I could do. I never realized I could tell a compelling story that would inspire people to step up and help me, until I did precisely that. I didn't know I could become an excellent wrestler until I continually put myself in a position where I needed to discover my strengths. I should have been a terrible wrestler. For a year, I *was* a terrible wrestler. Even when I finished high school, my technical abilities as a wrestler were extremely limited. Yet I discovered that what I had on other wrestlers my age was an ability to figure out what worked for me. My indomitable will to improve also helped. That was enough to carry me to the final match in the state championships, and it would have carried me to victory in that match if I hadn't allowed an anonymous trash-talker to turn my head.

If you want to achieve anything worthwhile in life, I encourage you to become a tryhard. Experiment until you discover your unique skills and what you have to offer the world. Figure out how to drive your life forward. When you know who you are, you can shape your reality.

This is a continual process, of course. There is no single definition of who you are and what your strengths are. Keep trying, keep learning, and keep evolving.

LEAVING FOR COLLEGE

By the end of high school, I had a scholarship with OIT, enough funds to purchase essential materials for college, and a Chevy LUV I purchased for five hundred dollars.

My cherished Chevy LUV, my first vehicle. I bought this when I was sixteen years old, through working evenings and weekends as a dishwasher.

Greg was going to Portland State. Before our lives diverged, we decided to take a trip down to California to see my dad, with a detour to San Francisco to visit my brother, Mark. I had a two-seater, three-cylinder Honda from the early 1970s, and we drove down to the town of Santa Rosa where my dad was living. On the way home, as we drove back north, the engine of the Honda blew up. We struggled to keep it moving until we reached the next town. We eventually pushed it to a junkyard in some northern California town where I sold it for twenty-five dollars to cover the bus fare back to Portland with Greg.

I had rigged a stereo in the Honda, so I salvaged the amplifier and the speakers, threw them into a duffle bag, and we both caught the bus from northern California to Portland, where Greg was already living. There was a bus from Portland to La Pine, but I missed it two days in a row because I was hauling a duffle bag that weighed hundreds of pounds. On the third day, I finally caught the bus and made it back to La Pine. By this time, I had only one day left to get to college in time.

My mom put together a care kit for me, which included a handful of Q-tips wrapped in aluminum foil, along with some other things she had scrounged from the house she thought might be useful. I threw some clothes in a bag and tossed the duffle bag full of speakers onto the back seat, fired up my Chevy LUV, and set off on the drive from La Pine to Klamath Falls.

Klamath Falls is relatively close to La Pine, about one-and-a-half to two hours down the I-97. As I dropped into the Klamath Basin, the terrain started to shift. High desert was replaced by flat, level woodland, primarily ponderosa pines. Klamath Lake itself is a wildlife preserve for the many species of birds that pass through the area. Klamath Falls was the largest place I had ever called home, populated by around twenty to thirty thousand people. OIT sits on the south side of Klamath Lake, a little north of Klamath Falls. From one side, the college offers a stunning view over the town and the lake. From the other, it opens onto treeless slopes and an unobstructed vista of the Klamath Basin.

When I first arrived in college, my roommate was a friend from high school. His presence provided me with a comforting reminder of the world I had left behind in La Pine. At the same time, I felt enormous relief knowing that I was moving into my own space. It was a place where I could write the next chapters of my life on my own, knowing that I would have time to study and that, if I earned money, it wouldn't disappear from the pocket of my pants. As I settled into my new room, I was slightly awestruck. I had made it to college.

CHAPTER SIX

NOVELTY

1995–2000 (AGE EIGHTEEN TO TWENTY-THREE), KLAMATH FALLS, OREGON

I didn't feel very good. I was anxious, on edge. My body was shaking. I knew I'd feel better soon, though. I stepped into the shower and felt the hot water pouring over my body. That had a cleansing and rejuvenating effect, albeit not as powerful an impact as the two beers I'd brought with me.

I'd been on a bender for several days. Coming off a major session was always tough, and I didn't feel ready to go cold turkey. I needed to taper off the alcohol. A morning shower with a couple of beers seemed like a good way to make myself feel a bit better before facing the day.

As I stood in the shower, drinking a beer and feeling the soothing effect of the water pouring over my head, I wondered how, within a couple of years of starting to drink, I had become so much like my parents. I never wanted that to happen. In fact, I didn't touch alcohol at all until I was almost nineteen years old, halfway through my freshman year in college, precisely *because* I was concerned about the alcoholism that ran in my family. Before I'd ever touched a drop, I feared that I might find it difficult to control my alcohol consumption. It turned out I was right. Soon, I was drinking far too much and far too long.

Beneath the surface anxieties, I felt as though I was dying. Somehow, I was following a path I had specifically decided that I wanted to avoid. My body felt terrible and I longed to escape the situation in which I found myself. As I leaned back against the wall of the shower, I wondered: am I trying to kill myself?

Depression issues have plagued my family for generations, creating a litany of suicides and early deaths. Was I doomed to repeat the same self-destructive behavior? Was I finding a way to punish myself for some perceived failures on my part, failures that only I could see?

Externally, my life looked great. I was twenty-one years old, about to turn twenty-two, and I was standing in the shower of a home I had purchased with money

I had earned. For all intents and purposes, I had finished college a year early, having completed almost two degrees. I worked full time as a production manager for a well-known window and door manufacturer, with responsibility for several supervisors and almost a hundred employees across several shifts. On the weekends, I ran my own small business through which I had formed a successful partnership with a small retail store in town. I was raising my oldest sister, who had moved down from La Pine to live with me in Klamath Falls.

It looked as though I had every reason to feel positive about life. Inside, however, I was falling apart. I didn't know where to turn. I only knew that, at the root of it, was my drinking. How did I get here? How could I get out?

THEME: THE POSITIVE AND NEGATIVE ASPECTS OF NEW EXPERIENCES

This chapter tells the story of my college years and the rest of my time in Klamath Falls. It describes my experiences as I forged an identity separate from my family, embracing the freedom to redefine myself. I discovered elements of my personality that I didn't know existed, and I also dredged up demons that had been lying in wait for me since I was a child.

During this time, I learned a great deal about the **positive**

and negative aspects of engaging with new experiences. For me, the changes were based on relocating and having the chance to interact with people who had no idea about my background. New experiences, however, can take many forms, from physical relocation to a career shift to moving into a new mental space, or anything else that shifts your current environment, internal or external.

In this chapter, you'll read about some drastic changes in my life, and come along for the ride as my professional life takes off. The period covered in this chapter features significant shifts both in my physical and emotional landscape. As you read it, reflect on times when you've made moves to alter your domain, either mental or physical, and what impact those shifts had on you.

A NEW ENVIRONMENT, A NEW IDENTITY

In college I totally reframed my self-perception, releasing many of the insecurities that plagued me through high school. It was only when I arrived at college and people treated me just the same as they treated everyone else that I realized how much I had been affected by the jibes that were part of the background noise in my high school days. The impact of those comments drove home the message that I didn't belong. In college, I suddenly felt as though I *did* belong. Everyone else was in the same boat. They too had moved from comfortable environments to a place that felt new, scary, and uncomfortable. In that context, I was normal.

My first couple of months in college were about meeting other people and figuring out who everybody was. Five or six of us, who were part of the engineering school, connected strongly and have remained friends to this day. One person in particular—Ben—had a habit of cutting classes on Fridays to take off home for the weekend. Ben had several interests at home, such as building vehicles and hunting, and he left college to focus on those interests.

In my mind, Ben was screwing up. I looked at him and saw someone who wasn't focused on his studies, and who didn't seem to care about his degree. I was convinced that he would flunk out within a year. In later years, I broached the subject with Ben. He told me that he thought exactly the same about me. Unbeknownst to me at the time, Ben noticed that I rarely went to classes, didn't purchase textbooks, and moved out of my dorm room within the first term. He thought I was blowing off college and felt sorry for my parents, imagining that they were paying for my education only to see me flame out.

Both Ben and I were completely wrong about each other. We went on to become two of the most successful people from our graduating class, both with advanced degrees and working in successful careers. To the untrained eye, it seemed as though we were slacking off. In fact, college for each of us was only one part of a much broader portfolio of activities and interests. Our seeming lack of commitment reflected our multidisciplinary approach to learning. Ben and I remain best friends and we still hang out frequently. He's an executive at an international tooling conglomerate and still lives only a short distance from me. A lot of our former engineering friends still approach us when they're looking for a new job. Not bad for a couple of failures.

HOW I STARTED DRINKING

Halfway through my first term in college, I decided I didn't want to continue living in my dorm room. People had told me that college would be harder than high school. I was fine with that. In fact, I had looked forward to it. For me, high school was incredibly boring. I was excited to test myself by studying tougher material. Within my first term at college, I was finding it no more difficult than high school and I was bored again.

The cost of living in Klamath Falls was exceptionally low. I determined that I could break my contract without losing a lot of money, so I moved into a house with three friends, all of whom also came to OIT from La Pine. I didn't need to spend a lot of time at school, so I moved out, cut my costs, and found a job. My roommates were fresh out of high school. Like many college freshmen, they drank alcohol regularly on evenings and weekends. At first, I avoided drinking, but before long I told myself that it couldn't hurt to have a few drinks with them from time to time.

I quickly discovered that I enjoyed drinking. In fact, I enjoyed drinking a *lot*. I liked the way it made me feel. I also liked the fact that it eased my social anxiety. I grew up living in tents, cabins, and—as the classic Chris Farley skits on *Saturday Night Live* would have it—a trailer down by the river. In my mind, everyone in La Pine had a story about who I was, and they judged me for my background.

At college, hardly anyone knew where I came from. I was in a new environment, where I could carve out a new identity for myself. Add alcohol and all of a sudden, I opened up. No longer did I feel different from everyone else. With a little bit of social lubrication, I discovered that I could be quite charismatic. That's what got me hooked.

I went from being someone who only talked to a few people, to being someone who was the life of the party. Everyone wanted to be around me and to talk to me. It was a very addictive experience. Very quickly, my alcohol consumption developed from a few casual drinks to a party every weekend. That soon grew into every weekend plus every Wednesday, which was a big bar night in Klamath Falls. From there, it progressed until drinking made up a huge portion of my life. I moved out of the house I shared with my friends from La Pine and into a big brick house on a hill, which became known as a party house. There's an old song from the 1970s named *Brick House*. It became our anthem, and the Brick House was the place to be for anyone in Klamath Falls looking for a party. Anyone who was looking for something to do, any evening of the week, knew that they could drop by the Brick House and something would be popping.

The switch flipped so fast I hardly knew myself. I went from not drinking at all to drinking heavily most nights of the week. Alcohol allowed me to forget myself and feel connected to everyone around me. It enabled me to tap into aspects of my personality I never knew existed. It was a huge contrast to my private, secluded upbringing, and I couldn't get enough of it.

Life at the Brick House was a lot of fun, but it wasn't a healthy environment for me to be in. It only encouraged me to drink. At one point, I drank every day for six months straight. Even my dad, who had struggled with alcoholism his whole life, expressed concern. He came to visit me, saw the walls of the house lined with empty bottles and told me he was worried that I was embarking on the same path he had been on.

Partying during college with my roommates at the Brick House.

Eventually, I realized it was time to leave the Brick House. One of my roommates and I left for a smaller, two-room place, with less partying and fewer temptations. I got back into lifting weights, two years after I had stopped. Partying, travel, work, and physical pain took their toll, deterring me from entering the gym for the longest period in my adult life. In high school, I hurt myself a few times, the worst being when I tore the ligaments connecting my collarbone to my sternum. This led to a lot of sharp pain in my chest, especially when I was cold or took deep breaths. To this day, my collarbone doesn't sit exactly where it's supposed to.

Without health insurance, I couldn't do much about it. Growing up, I saw injury and illness as part of life. Pat worked for years with a broken arm. My mom got into some bad scrapes, especially after she had been drinking, and she rarely went to the hospital. Although I noticed the problem, especially when I trained, living with pain and reduced mobility seemed normal to me.

There's no doubt that I took alcohol consumption too far. My drinking during this time period derailed several of my relationships and nearly cost me a job. I made several poor alcohol-induced choices that could have had a significant negative impact on the course of my life. I would *never* advocate that you follow my example in this area.

Nonetheless, I'm now at peace with that period of my life. I look at it as a learning experience that opened me up to a new understanding of my capabilities. Nowadays, I work as a speaker, presenter, and leader. I rely on my charisma to play the roles I've chosen in life. Alcohol could have had strongly negative consequences for me, but I live by the maxim that we should never regret our past, only learn from it.

Given my childhood experiences, I'm not sure that I would ever have been able to access the confidence to stand up in front of a room full of people if I hadn't first broken through some of the insecurities that I carried with me when I left La Pine for Klamath Falls. I drank too much, to the point where it created significant issues in my life, but I can't deny that it also opened me up to aspects of my personality that could otherwise have remained dormant indefinitely.

PARTY GUY OR SMARTEST KID IN THE CLASS?

Given how much I drank, most of my peers assumed that I was flunking college. Based on my attendance records, it seemed like they were right. Every term, I started out with good intentions. I told myself that *this* term I would get my shit together, buy all my textbooks, and attend classes. I headed over to the college bookshop, bought a full set of books, and—for the first couple of weeks—showed up for class. It didn't take long for my good intentions to go out of the window.

In my defense, I was frustrated by the quality of the syllabus. I sat in class, listened to the teacher, and glanced at the homework assignments. My budget was tight, and I had no backup plan. Unlike many of my peers, I had zero financial support from my parents. There was no one I could call for a loan if I ran out of money. It didn't take me long to conclude that I could find something much better to do with five hundred dollars than spend it on textbooks.

The college bookshop allowed students to return books within two weeks of purchase for a full refund. After that, books were considered secondhand, and they were worth a fraction of their original value. Every term, days before the two-week deadline, I found myself returning to the store and claiming refunds on the books I had bought.

One of the reasons the bookshop offered this service was to prevent kids who changed classes from winding up with books they no longer needed. I made use of those first two weeks for another purpose: I assessed my classes based on their homework demands.

There were two types of instructor at OIT. Some assigned required homework, others assigned recommended homework. You can probably guess which classes I sought out. If I found myself in a class with required homework, I dropped it and moved to one with recommended homework.

It was easy to tell that the professors were working from a similar course syllabus because the overall content of the classes were similar. The homework consisted of the same assignments. The only difference was that when I took classes with recommended homework, I knew I wouldn't have to do it.

Fortunately for me, I was extremely good at tests. This is not to say that I was smarter than other people in the room. We all have a unique way of operating, and I constantly meet people who are smarter than me in their area of expertise. I happen to be good at tests. *Really* good.

Another factor influencing my sporadic attendance in college was the lack of reliable transportation. I lived off campus and whenever my vehicle broke down, which was frequently, it was difficult for me to get to school. There were some bus lines in Klamath Falls, but they didn't run regularly. I lived close enough to work to walk in, but college was too far to walk.

Many of my work and partying friends thought that I didn't go to college at all. To a lot of people, I was one of those funny, goofy guys whose life revolved around partying. They saw—or thought they saw—me skating through college, taking a class here or there. In fact, I took nineteen to twenty-one credits per term. Twelve credits was considered a full-time load.

That perception started to change in my junior year. By this time, I was taking some senior year classes as well as my junior year ones. Certain classes were deemed especially significant, and there was one in particular—Strength and Materials, for example—that freaked everyone out.

There were a couple of reasons for this. First, it was an exceptionally challenging class. Second, it was one of the most important things people hiring engineering graduates looked at. The class was viewed as such a key indicator of a person's ability that employers were more interested in how students fared in this class than in someone's overall grade point average (GPA). Because it was such a challenging class, it was common for students to receive Cs and Ds.

Strength and Materials was compulsory. The homework was compulsory too. To meet the college's graduation requirements, I needed to buy the course textbooks and turn in the homework. Each week, homework consisted of a single problem. Most people got together in groups of four or five and spent hours working on the homework during the week. I took a different approach.

I showed up at the beginning of each class, broke out my notebook, and started working. After about ten minutes, I would hand in the few lines I'd written. At first, this earned me some strange looks from people who had spent hours working on the problem and handed in three to five pages. It wasn't unusual for people to ask, "What the hell are you doing?"

Every week, my homework turned out to be correct. It shifted the way people saw me a lot.

By my junior year, I had completed all my coursework for one degree, and all but about nine credits of a second engineering degree. All I needed to do was complete my senior project and I would have one degree, plus the majority of another. I picked up an internship with a window manufacturing company in my junior year, which turned into full-time professional employment when I was in my senior year.

At this point, I wasn't going to school very much. My senior project was still in progress. I needed to decide whether to take the last few credits of my second degree. And I was president of the engineering society, which came about as the result of a joke. Most of my peers saw me as a fun, goofy guy who liked to party. It wasn't until I began to ace difficult classes that they began to realize I was top of the class. Most people assumed I was hardly engaged, a whisker from dropping out.

When the time came to elect the president of the engineering society, someone suggested voting for Kabuki—my nickname. A big group of students wrote in their votes for me, never for a moment believing that I would be elected. But I was.

The role worked out well for me. My job was to allocate some of our chapter's financial resources, enhance the experience of our members, and coordinate events. I arranged some great trips, such as tours of related industrial facilities in the Pacific Northwest.

In my last year, many of my fellow students shifted

their perceptions of me significantly, to the extent that I became something of a folk legend among my peers. In their minds, I lived like I was in the movie *Animal House*, rarely attended school, and didn't purchase any books, yet somehow I had the highest graduating engineering GPA in my year group. Nonetheless, I would never claim to be the smartest guy in the room. I'm good at tests and I know my strengths, so I positioned myself to succeed.

HOME FOR THE SUMMER

During my first couple of years in college, I occasionally made the two-and-a-half-hour drive home to work weekends at the resort in Sun River. Over the summers, I did longer stints working full time either busing or waiting tables, saving up a substantial amount of money.

It was while waiting tables that I discovered I have an unusual ability to visualize connections. This skill, along with my ability to excel on tests, allowed me to do well in college. More recently, it's a superpower I've called on many times to develop what has become Kabuki Strength.

I found that I could visualize the entire dining room, including every order, right down to how much water was in each person's glass. I didn't use a notepad. I had an internal picture of how quickly every diner was consuming their food and drink. This allowed me to make quite a lot of money, because I was able to serve many tables at once.

Testing myself became a fun, challenging sport for me, much like playing a video game. As other waiters started to freak out, they handed me one of their tables. I kept taking on more and more tables, to see how far I could push it. By close of business, I was usually working half the dining room, while the other half was split between three or four other waiters. It was an experience that clued me into the fact that my ability to visualize scenes and connections is highly unusual.

My parents knew that I was working. If I saw them, they asked me for money, so I chose not to go home. Instead, I camped out with some friends, outside La Pine and Sun River. From years of living in the area, I knew all the best camping spots. In fact, I wound up revisiting many of my childhood haunts as an adult. My first move when I returned home to familiar terrain was to pitch a tent in a spot I knew as a kid.

Those first two summers back from college were a lot of fun. I worked with my old high school friends and we partied by the river at night. Looking back, there was a part of me that still wanted to maintain the connections that linked me with La Pine and Sun River. I hadn't fully accepted that I was building a life of my own, separate and distinct from the life I had known prior to leaving.

By my junior year, however, my mentality had shifted. Klamath Falls felt like home and I no longer felt the same pull to return north.

COMBINING COLLEGE AND WORK

Throughout college, I worked at a job that evolved into a full-time role. As mentioned earlier, during my junior year, I was hired as an intern for a door and window manufacturer. The company was a huge, multibillion-dollar organization that owned several major assets in the area. It was easily the largest business in Klamath Falls.

A role with the company was considered a premium placement because it was a secure job with excellent benefits. Even people who worked in production, a relatively low-level position, were respected within the community. When I arrived as an intern, I expected to work under a manager whose job it was to train me.

Within two weeks of my arrival, however, he was promoted to one of the company's facilities in California. When he received this news, he vanished. I never saw him again. Two weeks into an internship, I suddenly found myself managing his team of thirty to forty people, all of whom were long-term employees. Most had been with the company for several decades, yet they were expected to answer to me, many years their junior and totally inexperienced. My promotion occurred partly by default. The manager above me was still technically supposed to be mentoring me, but when he left, he was never replaced. I was performing the job well, so I simply stepped up in his place.

It was a trial by fire, to say the least. I stayed on and managed the crew for about a year, all the while being paid as an intern. Then, a scandal broke. Several employees accused their peers of harassment, which triggered an internal investigation. Over the course of the investigation, it became clear that there were a lot of unethical activities taking place at the plant. This led to the firing of approximately half the plant's managers. The general manager, who had been in his position for about twenty years, was reassigned to a department known as "special projects." Moving someone to special projects is a euphemistic way of shunting them out of sight when they have incurred disciplinary action or performed poorly, but they're too experienced, respected, or connected to fire.

Naturally, the company hired a lot of new staff and a new general manager, who came from another state. For some time, the environment was highly stressful and chaotic, especially for those of us in a management position. No one was certain what to expect, or who knew what. Some people were attempting to cover their tracks, in the hope that their role in the unethical practices that had been uncovered would go unnoticed.

In my very early twenties, I was caught in the crossfire. When the period of my internship was up, I met with the new general manager and he offered me a job. In the circumstances, he asked me whether I was certain I wanted to accept the role. I did so without hesitation, which appeared to surprise him. As I look back now, I think that no sane person would have been willing to take on a managerial role in a company in the midst of so much drama, with so many members of staff losing their jobs. I think that because I grew up surrounded by chaos, I found it easy to accept the situation in which I found myself. It seemed normal to me.

I was placed in charge of a different department. As I watched how the plant was run, I noticed a huge opportunity to improve on the operational side of the business. I put together a proposal and presented it to the new general manager, and he agreed to give it a try. The improvements worked. Prior to enacting my suggestions, it took us months to turn raw materials into the engineered component we shipped out to window assembly plants. Afterward, the lead time was cut to weeks.

Recognizing the success of my initiative, the general manager came back to me and asked me to take over two more departments, apply a similar process, and come back to him with recommendations. My proposal involved integrating the two departments and streamlining workflow, a move that proved equally successful. The next thing I knew, at the age of twenty-one, I had a third of the largest manufacturing plant in Klamath Falls reporting to me. I was responsible for a hundred employees, three managers, and three supervisors who oversaw the three different shifts I managed.

By this time, product throughput was down to days, sometimes even hours. The plant had existed since the late 1960s with little process innovation. By improving throughput, we succeeded in significantly reducing inventory levels, creating millions of dollars in positive impact for the company.

The whole experience gave me a new perspective on myself. I was only twenty-one and I still had a limited amount of social confidence. I still saw myself as quite an introverted person—except when I was drinking—and I didn't fully understand how I was able to succeed. Technically, I was still in college, although with the exception of my senior project, I had the credits to graduate. I was able to generate a significant positive impact for both the company and the employees, and I loved it. I enjoyed the feeling of leadership and the sense of purpose that came with fixing problems and improving processes. I found it fascinating and rewarding to be an agent of change.

Simultaneously, my experiences convinced me that I never wanted to work as an engineer. I realized that I wasn't interested in sitting at a computer for hours on end, drawing parts, jigs, and fixtures. I wanted to be a leader.

I didn't think I had the right personality to be a leader, though. I thought leaders were supposed to be outspoken and extroverted, delivering motivational speeches and inspiring people with force of personality. By this time, I had taken custody of the first of my three sisters and had started a paintball business in my spare time. With these two factors in mind, along with the fact that I enjoyed what I was doing, I made the decision not to take the final nine credits that would have secured my second engineering degree.

Instead, I began to nurture an ambition to get a master's degree in management or business.

A VEHICLE SUITABLE FOR THE CITY OF SUNSHINE

Klamath Falls is known as the City of Sunshine. The town receives more days of sunshine than any other town in Oregon. When I reached a stage where I was working full time at a large window manufacturer, and I owned my own house, I decided that I wanted to purchase a vehicle that reflected my growing self-confidence. I had always made do with cheap, five-hundred-dollar cars, which served a purpose, but frequently broke down. I browsed the classified ads and I decided that I wanted a Jeep. I was living in the sunniest city in Oregon, I had the money to buy a vehicle I genuinely wanted, so I settled on a badass Jeep.

I picked up a 1976 Jeep CJ-7 for a reasonable price. I loved it. It had big tires, and with all the sunshine, I kept the top off all year. It was a perfect vehicle to take out paint-balling, with my paintballing gear in a trailer attached to the back, or to bounce around the dirt roads outside of town.

One day, I was backing into my driveway and the front axle broke clean in half. The center of the axle was on the ground and the tires were cocked out to the side. A rush of adrenaline passed through me as I realized how lucky I was that the axle hadn't broken when I was driving along the highway. Nonetheless, the experience gave me my first taste of modifying vehicles, a world I would revisit many times over the years. I paid a visit to a Jeep builder in town, who happened to have an axle he was taking out of his own Jeep. It was a much bigger, stronger axle than the one that had broken on me, so I purchased it. He explained to me how to lift the vehicle and install the new axle, which I did successfully, fitting some thirty-five-inch tires for good measure. It was the beginning of my interest in customizing and fabricating vehicles.

A PAINTBALL BUSINESS ON THE SIDE

As though I didn't have enough to focus on, I had also started my own paintball business. As mentioned in the previous chapter, I played paintball regularly in high school. During my first few years in college, I stayed in touch with my old paintball buddies and we traveled to compete in tournaments. We rented and bought all our paintball equipment from the same guy, and I decided to reach out to him and ask him whether he was interested in selling his business.

Turned out, he was.

I bought thirty rental guns, all the equipment I needed to run a paintball rental business, and the licenses I needed to purchase supplies on a wholesale basis. A friend of mine owned a couple of storefronts in Klamath Falls, and he agreed to set up all my products in one of his stores so his staff could sell it. Over the weekends, I took groups of people out and created team-building paintball games, an offering that became popular with local companies. It was a mixture of work and play and I enjoyed it a lot.

TAKING CUSTODY OF MY ELDEST SISTER

Soon after I moved out of the Brick House, I heard from my oldest sister, Melissa. Our mom had undergone a mental breakdown. My mom was at work waiting tables, and she lost control of herself. She began pacing in circles in the middle of the dining room, muttering to herself. No one could snap her out of it, so someone called mental health services to come and get her. Although she did recover from that episode, she disappeared soon after. When I spoke to her in later years, she explained that she couldn't handle living with Pat, who was still spending his days sitting around the house, drinking. The frustration and violence finally tipped her over the edge. She took off to Montana and none of us saw her for several years.

All three of my sisters were living at home with Pat. Unfortunately, by this time in his life, Pat was on a downward spiral from which he would never recover. When he met my mom, he was a heroin addict and a burglar. For a while, their partnership kept him relatively clean. As their relationship deteriorated, however, along with his health, his condition declined.

Living with Pat was a terrible environment for my sisters. The house was filthy and should have been condemned, and Pat was in no condition to provide parenting. One winter, he accused Melissa of stealing his favorite cereal bowl and kicked her out into the snow. She bounced around for a week or so and gravitated toward a drug house in Portland, about four hours north of La Pine on the other side of the Cascade Range of mountains. When she called me, she knew that she needed to get out, but she didn't know where to go. Meanwhile, my other sisters also moved away. My middle sister, Janis, had gotten herself into a little bit of trouble and found herself in the care of the state. My youngest sister, Amy, was living with the parents of one of her close friends.

When Melissa called me, I told her to come to Klamath Falls and live with me. I was able to contact our mom and complete the paperwork that allowed me to take custody of Melissa. I was twenty-one years old at the time.

In my senior year, I purchased a house that Melissa and I shared, with no other roommates. Although my alcohol consumption was down from its peak, I was still drinking a lot. In my mind, I felt it was justified because I was working so hard. I used to tell Melissa that I had earned the right to party because I was creating the environment in which she lived. Undoubtedly, I could have set a better example, but that was the best I could do at the time.

Melissa made a lot of progress in those years. She worked toward her General Educational Development (GED) tests, learned how to drive, and secured a job. Sitting in the passenger seat while she drove made me fear for my own safety, so I gave her a vehicle and let her figure it out on her own. Nonetheless, she passed her test and got her license.

Me and my sisters. Melissa and Janis were living independently by this time, while Amy was still under my care.

CONSCIOUSLY RECREATING MY ENVIRONMENT

My two-year break from training had allowed my collarbone to heal enough that I was able to train without incurring significant pain, which I did several days per week. I was working full time, running my paintball business, and taking care of Melissa. Despite these responsibilities, I continued to party hard. I was so well known as a party animal that the parties were following me around. Sometimes I would arrive home from work, ready to chill, only to find that a group of people had shown up at my house with a keg and a party was in full swing.

My drinking was still out of control. I would go on a bender over the weekends, hiding my alcohol consumption while I hosted events on Saturdays, and stayed mostly clean during the week. Even so, the effects lingered. It took two, sometimes three, days at the gym before my sweat stopped smelling of alcohol. By Thursday and Friday, I began to feel better, but then I repeated the cycle. This pattern was aggravated by the stress of my job, and the pressure I felt from the assistant plant manager to take even more steps forward. The more stressed I felt, the more I drank. Eventually, I realized that I could no longer function in the environment. I knew I had to find a way out.

As I was wrestling with my demons, my middle sister, Janis, contacted me. She was recently released from the juvenile detention facility in which she had been living, and was unwilling to move back in with Pat. She asked whether she could move in with me. Although I was already spending most of what I earned, leaving me with few spare funds, her request functioned as a catalyst. I decided that, if I was going to handle my drinking, I needed to leave Klamath Falls. I had created an environment in which I was constantly surrounded by triggers. It was time to leave that environment and move elsewhere.

Although I wasn't sure how I would make the mortgage payments, I told Melissa that the house was hers. By this point, she had been living with me for a few years and had turned eighteen, so she was in a position to contribute to the mortgage payments. I gave my employer notice that I intended to leave and set about making plans to find a job in Portland. I was in a leadership role at work and it was my company's practice not to retain people in leadership positions after receiving notice, so they let me go the day I gave them my notice. I jumped into my Jeep and drove to Portland.

LESSON: THE PARADOX OF NOVELTY

There are both positive and negative aspects of walking into a new environment. One of the positives is that a new place can translate into a new start. If you wish to separate yourself from experiences that no longer reflect who you are, a change of location can be an excellent opportunity to do that. Putting yourself into a fresh setting, with a blank slate, makes it much easier to recreate yourself.

That's where I was when I left La Pine for Klamath Falls. I needed to put distance between myself and the existence I knew so that I could begin to build the foundations of the rest of my life. That was much easier to do without the insecurities and the sense of isolation that had dogged me when I was in La Pine.

On the other hand, moving to a new place can be scary

and unpredictable. As much as it offers an opportunity for reinvention, it can also lead you into unexpected risks and consequences. The more unfamiliar a situation, the more freedom it offers you to redefine yourself. At the same time, that lack of familiarity strips away the anchors that keep you safe, which can lead you to make poor choices.

Let's acknowledge, too, that we can't simply run away from everything that disturbs us. There's a distinction between purposely placing yourself in a new environment, with the intention of enacting change, and running away from painful situations or emotions. While I certainly did a lot of the former while I was at college, I did some of the latter, too. For example, I didn't know how to relate to my family. I avoided spending time with them, even when I was back in La Pine or Sun River. This seemed to have consequences for everyone else in my family, too. For reasons I still don't fully understand, my presence appeared to stabilize the volatile personalities of those I was closest to. As soon as I left, the situation at home began to decline rapidly. Within a couple of years, the family unit that I had thought was the most secure part of my life had completely fallen apart.

Another element of my life that came with me to Klamath Falls was my family history of alcoholism and depression. Indeed, they expressed themselves strongly while I was at college, forcing me to find ways of coming to terms with them. I made negative choices, and I knew at the time they were negative. For example, a big part of me understood that drinking alcohol wasn't going to work out well for me. I was in a new space, however, and I convinced myself that a few drinks here and there wouldn't pose a problem.

If you choose to put yourself in a new situation, embrace the positive opportunities it offers you. Think through what you want to accomplish before you make the move, so you understand your motivations and have a strong chance to manage your behavior. Nonetheless, be aware of the risks that come with uprooting yourself. Recognize when you are moving somewhere new because you want to accomplish something valuable, and when you are looking to escape your problems. The second approach, unfortunately, rarely succeeds.

FROM THE EAGLE TO THE DRAGON

When I was nineteen years old, I decided to get my first tattoo. It's a large work, starting at my ankle, working up, and covering both my stomach and a significant portion of my back. The tattoo depicts two eagles, one on the front of my body and one on the back, each with a chain around its ankle. The eagles are attempting to take flight, but they can't, because they're both shackled to *my* ankle. I came up with this design because it symbolizes my belief that we can accomplish whatever we desire in life, and the only thing holding us back is ourselves.

Every day, the eagles on my body remind me to realize my full potential. If I could distill the narrative of my childhood and adolescence into a single theme, I'd say it's a story about overcoming extraordinary odds. I was born into unusual and challenging circumstances, and for many of my early years, I had little or no control over my life. Even in college, where I was beginning to lay the groundwork for the life I live today, I felt as though a lot of the things I experienced were happening *to* me. I wasn't the architect.

Up to this point in my life, my reinvention wasn't wholly purposeful. I was beginning to understand my strengths and realize what I'm capable of, but I wasn't exerting conscious effort. I was still largely going with the flow. I didn't have a plan to help me decide who, where, and how I wanted to be. In the first half of my life, I encountered and overcame obstacles when they hit me, learning all the time about who I was and what I could do. In the second half of my life—and this book—the focus shifts toward conscious, deliberate reinvention.

PART TWO

THE DRAGON

CHAPTER SEVEN

———————————

BUILDING

2000–2008 (AGE TWENTY-THREE TO THIRTY-ONE), PORTLAND, OREGON

My Jeep served me well for my mile-long commute in Klamath Falls, where there was sunshine almost every day of the year. For long-distance travel, it was less useful. It was more than twenty years old and, since I lifted the wheels, it had a tendency to veer across the road. The engine—a giant V8—was heavy on the fuel consumption. I left my other vehicle—a Chevy Blazer that would have been a far more practical choice of transportation—with my sister Melissa.

With my Jeep, I drove the four hundred miles from Klamath Falls to Portland to start fresh.

Four hundred miles may seem like a minor trip. The journey, however, required three tanks of gas. As I drove over the mountains, wind whistled through the one-inch gaps in the doors and the hardtop. The Jeep didn't have a defrosting mechanism, so I kept a rag beside me to wipe the windows down and maintain visibility.

When I pulled into downtown Portland, I was met by Greg, my friend from high school. Greg was finishing his degree at Portland State and living in an apartment downtown. I parked my Jeep in his parking garage and crashed at his place for two weeks.

We didn't have a lot of money between us, but we got by. Every morning, we ate bacon and eggs for breakfast. Then, he left for school while I sat at the computer and started hammering out resumés and scheduling interviews. As an engineer with management experience in a hot market, I was in high demand. Within a couple of weeks, I had multiple interviews lined up, and my pick of jobs. I quickly picked one as a production manager for a manufacturer of high-tech circuit boards, and I took out a lease on a duplex.

Those first two weeks, however, involved a lot of soul searching. I had walked away from a secure, well-paying job to come to Portland with no guarantees and few resources. I had the following month's mortgage payment sitting in my bank account, but beyond that I had hardly any financial resources to call on. Crashing on Greg's couch, with no permanent place to live, I began questioning my choices. I wasn't sure how I would take care of myself, let alone my sister Melissa in Klamath Falls.

Despite these doubts, deep down I felt good about my decision. I knew that back in Klamath Falls, I would never have found it within myself to dial back my drinking. The pull of the environment was too strong. In new circumstances, however, I succeeded in reducing my alcohol consumption to one to three drinks per week, where it has stayed ever since. I moved from the far south of the state to the far north, from a small country town to the largest city in Oregon. It was a huge change.

As I sat in the new space and walked around the city blocks, I felt as though I had undergone another major shift, this time more deliberately. I had separated myself from family and college and placed myself in an entirely new environment, and I had choice. I could choose where to work. I could decide what influences I would bring into my life. I could select which friends I wanted to stay in touch with. The new environment felt like a catalyst. Within a month of moving to Portland, I had joined a gym, secured a new job, signed a lease, and submitted an application to study for an MBA.

When I had a foothold in Portland, I was able to take custody of Janis, who came to live with me in my duplex. For the first two years in the city, my life was defined by the grind. I worked, I trained seven days a week, I studied for my MBA. I also did what I could to take care of Janis, although I placed a heavy emphasis on helping her to become self-reliant. She got her GED and started working.

Moving to Portland precipitated a total shift in my life. Even before I left Klamath Falls, I was a highly driven person and I spent a lot of time working and learning. When I moved to Portland, however, I took those qualities to another level. Relocating gave me a clean break and allowed me to pour almost my entire focus into productive activities.

THEME: BUILDING FOR THE FUTURE

This chapter is about mastering new skills and using them to construct a successful life. When we decide to build something, we need to take responsibility for the fruits of our labor, even when some elements of the process lie outside our direct control. This may involve hard work and difficult decisions. **Building** something great, however, is not merely an additive process. We also need to pare away those things that aren't serving us, perhaps activities that are fun and enjoyable, but which don't move us closer to our true objectives.

When we walk through this fire, we forge an identity of our own choosing. This is distinct from an identity that's thrust upon us. Building anything worthwhile requires a tremendous degree of self-leadership. This may or may not mean standing in front of an audience. It can simply be the discipline to show up every day at a task that's contributing to a larger goal.

In this day and age, it sometimes seems as though there is a tendency for people to blame circumstances or other people for their lack of success. It's easy to focus on the bad things that have happened to us but, ultimately, we're still responsible for our own actions. Only we have the power to select our path, separate ourselves from influences that drag us down, and reshape our lives. The stories you'll find in this chapter reflect these themes.

THE DRAGON COMES INTO FOCUS

So far, this book has focused on the eagle attempting to take flight. I hope it has inspired you to begin realizing your full potential. This chapter, however, signifies a shift to the influence of the dragon, the Ouroboros. As described in the introduction, my second tattoo surrounds my entire upper body. It's a circular design and it represents the renewal or recreation of life. As we consume our own past, we reinvent ourselves.

Unlike the eagles, however, straining to break the chains that bind them, the Ouroboros implies death and rebirth in full awareness of what we're doing. It doesn't only ask us what we can achieve; it asks what we *want* to achieve. What do we choose to create? Who do we choose to become?

This is an exciting and scary process. Unless you're excited about the vision you choose to pursue, why would you invest time and energy into it? If it's truly meaningful, it will push you beyond your comfort zone. To be worthy of you, your goal will inevitably ask new questions of you and take you to places you've never previously visited, emotionally, psychologically, and perhaps literally.

Achieving valuable goals takes time. It's unlikely that, when you embark along a path of work, you will see immediate results. In hindsight, some of the events in this chapter formed the foundations of the life I live today. At the time, however, that wouldn't have been obvious. Even I wouldn't have guessed that ramping up my training would one day lead to me becoming one of the strongest people in the world. I didn't know that going back to school and studying for an MBA would be a step on the road toward becoming a corporate executive and turning around failing companies. This is all true, and I don't believe I could have reached the place where I am today without these years of fundamental building.

MY PROFESSIONAL LIFE MOVES TO THE NEXT LEVEL

For my first three years in Portland, I worked with the manufacturer of high-tech circuit boards. I progressed to running a business unit within the company, managing seventy-five employees and six shift supervisors. Although I continued to question my own suitability for leadership, I understood that whatever I was doing was working. A lot of my leadership style involved engaging everyone who worked under me on a one-to-one basis. I made sure to explain my vision to them and let them know how they fit into it. I also took the time to solicit their ideas and feedback.

Over the course of those three years, I succeeded in reducing total labor cost by nearly half for every hole we drilled into our circuit boards, and in improving safety around the plant. Most significantly, however, I shrunk the physical size of the business unit to half its original dimensions. This involved bringing equipment and assembly stations much closer together. At first, people were resistant. They felt that they needed more space to work efficiently. As I explained my thinking, however, and we tested out the first iteration of the new space, it became clear that the redesign made everyone's job easier.

When the first size reduction proved successful, I started a second iteration, then a third. Contracting our operations into such a compact space left a lot of unused space in the factory, which I segregated with cones and tape to keep it clear. By the third year of my tenure, I had created a gigantic free space in the middle of the manufacturing plant where I worked.

This creation of space turned out to be a huge boon. The company owned two manufacturing facilities in Portland and times were tough. The dot-com bubble had burst and manufacturers across the country were overstocked with inventory. After attempting to weather the storm, the company decided to tackle the problem by consolidating operations and laying off staff. The space I had freed up through reducing the size of our business unit suddenly presented a huge opportunity. The organization shut down its other manufacturing facility and moved it into the empty space I had created.

Needing to shed staff, the company offered employees the opportunity to take voluntary layoffs. After three years of busting my ass, I thought this was a great idea. I was finally in a position where my level of responsibility was on the decline. Melissa was living independently in Klamath Falls. I had finished my MBA, Janis had moved out, married, and become pregnant, and I had saved enough money to take an entire year off. My plan was to load my Jeep up on a trailer and take off to Mexico, where I would spend a year off-roading and camping. I was so excited to have some fun.

I applied for a voluntary layoff, received approval, and was ready to go. Then I was told that I needed to stay on for an additional three to four months in order to manage the integration of the new business unit into our facility. I took on this responsibility, along with managing the shutdown of the company's other location across town.

The whole process had a long-term positive impact on the company, setting it up for success in the wake of the dot-com crash. It was also a great experience for me. By the time I left that organization, I had become comfortable with my personal leadership style, despite the fact that it was different from the way I initially thought I *should* lead. I was highly confident that I had the skills to unite employees in the service of common goals, deliver change, and execute solutions at an exceptionally high level. While my working life was progressing fast, however, the family I knew was falling apart.

HOW'S THE FAMILY?

Meanwhile, my mom was still cycling in and out of mental crises. Unfortunately, she was in contact with my sisters at this time and some of her behavior still has a negative impact on them to this day. Pat was living in absolute squalor and drinking himself to death.

Prior to coming to live with me in Portland, Janis spent

some time in a juvenile detention center. Mark, my brother, was in prison and would be for a decade to come. The choice he made to live with his father and stepmother scarred the rest of his life. By the age of fourteen he was doing crystal meth at home with his parents. By eighteen he was in prison, never having fully experienced adolescence or adulthood. In later years, he confessed that he has been plagued with mental health issues, both from these episodes and due to the guilt he carries with him as a result of the lies he told in court about being molested in our household.

My biological father was clean and sober while this was going on, although he had burned through the remaining money he had earned from the sale of his parents' properties. Therefore, he was living in a low-income apartment complex in Santa Rosa.

My older cousin, John, became a prostitute in San Francisco, contracted AIDS, and died. Stoney, his younger brother, disappeared. To this day, we've never heard from him again. I can only guess that he died. My mom's sister, Stoney and John's mother, embezzled my great-grandma's retirement savings. She too disappeared and we've never heard from her again. I imagine that her addictions got the better of her and she has passed away.

It was obvious to me that, if I didn't bust my ass to take

care of myself and my sisters, no one else would. I was all they had.

TWO CHRISTMASES, TWO FAREWELLS

It was the Friday prior to Christmas 2002. I was in the gym training, as I did every day by this time in my life. I had finished my final sets for the day, and I was sitting in the locker room, getting ready to change back into my street clothes. With Christmas around the corner, I was planning a vacation and looking forward to a week off.

My phone rang. It was the Santa Rosa Sheriff's Department. I picked up and spoke to the sheriff. He told me that my biological father had passed away.

As I listened, the sheriff explained that my father had actually died a few weeks earlier, but it had taken a while for the sheriff's department to locate contact information for his next of kin. As the only remaining family member, the sheriff asked me to head back to Santa Rosa and take care of my father's personal effects. I hung up the phone and sat down on the bench in the gym locker room, digesting what I had just heard.

Canceling my vacation, I jumped on a flight and flew into San Francisco. My childhood friend Ganya drove a couple of hours to pick me up from the airport and transport me to his parents' house. They had moved off the mountain—although Ganya was working on building his own homestead on the property where we had lived as children—and I stayed with them for a few days, using their home as a base. From there, I drove to my father's apartment complex in Santa Rosa.

At the time of his death, my father shared an apartment. He had spent most of his money and he was living in a low-income complex, populated mainly by recovering addicts and alcoholics, so sharing was part of the deal. The guy he lived with hadn't been a close friend, but I stopped to talk to him, and he told me about my father's last hours.

My dad's roommate said that he had been sitting on the couch talking to my dad one morning. He got up and went into his room. When he came back out to the living room a few hours later, my father was still sitting in the same position, but he had passed away, of heart failure.

My father had suffered from heart problems for a while before he died. A few weeks prior, he had apparently undergone an operation to put in a stent. Following his release from the hospital, tests showed no abnormalities and he was recovering at home. Sadly, his heart wasn't as strong as his doctors had believed.

I stood in my father's apartment, surveying the few things

he owned. He died with little to his name, and I couldn't bring myself to take possession of what he left. Instead, I took everything to the commons area of the apartment complex and let everyone there know they could take what they wanted. For the people who lived there, my father's books and other worldly goods were a bonanza.

When I was taking care of my father's effects, I found all the drawings and letters I sent him in a suitcase in his apartment. He had kept every single one. He printed out every email I ever sent him and filed it away. They formed a detailed record of what was happening in my life over the course of years, reminding me of events and stories that I had long since forgotten. I spent hours reading through them and dissolving into a mess of tears. I also found a letter from my mother, sent while she was in jail, telling him not to come after me. It struck me as a powerful example of both her strength and her determination to get her way.

My letters to my father—along with his own writings—are the only things I have kept as a memento of our relationship. He was a prolific writer who penned his reflections on his travels and always anticipated that he would one day write a book. Although he never succeeded in that goal, I found a large box of both typed and handwritten pieces in his home after his death, that he had hoped to publish one day.

He had an old station wagon from the early 1970s, with stickers from South America plastered to the bumper and a big set of cow horns tied to the front hood. I loaded his writings and his guitar into the Volvo, jumped in, and made the long, slow drive back to Portland. I still had some remaining vacation, so I took a week for the drive, visiting friends along the route.

My father, Daniel, in Santa Rosa, California, with his Volvo. Note the cow horns tied to the hood.

My father's death stirred something in me. During the summer of 2003, I decided to go visit Pat. I scheduled a trip with friends and did some four wheeling in the central Oregon mountains, driving my Jeep off-road before landing in La Pine to see my stepfather.

We met outside the old mobile home where I'd lived when I was in high school. He didn't invite me in, probably because both he and the home had deteriorated significantly since I'd last seen him. After his death, I found out that he had converted much of the house into grow rooms, by covering the floor with dirt and setting up a small weed-growing operation.

Despite his poor condition, and the poor condition of the mobile home, it was good to see him. As always, he was in great spirits. He seemed oblivious to the hardships of his situation—to the filth of his home and the lack of a vehicle. He had a bicycle, and he used to load his pockets with beers, carry his fishing pole in one hand, and cycle down to the river almost every day. There he would spend his days fishing and drinking. Although his sanity levels had slipped further, he seemed happy.

Pat was so pleased to have me around that he took me to see a couple of his friends to show me off. Bizarrely, his friends—both of whom had spent time behind bars— kept telling me that, due to my size, I wouldn't have any problems if I wound up in prison. They continued to repeat this assertion even after I assured them that I had no intention of taking my life in that direction, and that fighting wasn't the purpose behind my training.

The following December, a year almost to the day since I had received the call informing me of my father's death, I was in the locker room of the exact same gym. Once again, I had just finished my workout. I had just completed my last shift before Christmas, and I was looking forward to taking a week off. As I pulled my street clothes out of my locker, my phone rang. This time it was the sheriff's department from central Oregon.

The sheriff on the other end of the line told me that Pat had passed away. He explained that, although he knew I wasn't a blood relative, he was led to believe I was the best person to take care of Pat's affairs. The sheriff told me that Pat was sitting on his couch, in front of the television, just like my father a year earlier. Even more strangely, it seemed that Pat, too, died of heart failure. The story of Pat's death was nearly identical to the story of my father's death, a year apart.

I drove to Oregon to meet my sisters, who had taken the lead organizing Pat's cremation. I never asked them to do that and I was proud of them for taking the initiative. At this time, I was about a month from packing up and leaving for Mexico. My youngest sister, Amy, however, found herself in a difficult situation. For a number of years, she had been officially under Pat's care, while actually living with friends. With his passing, that illusion could no longer be sustained. Unless I stepped in, she would become a ward of the state, so I took custody of her, too.

Pat's death brought my father's death into sharper focus. Although I was less deeply involved in the practical aspects of handling Pat's affairs, it sparked a lot of emotions. I watched my sisters process the death of their father and listened to the stories they shared—some joyful, some wacky, some flat-out insane. The emotions these stories provoked were an extraordinary mix. It was clear that Pat had loved his daughters deeply, yet he had also bequeathed them a lot of pain.

As I reflected on the roles both Pat and my father had played in my life, I found myself thinking about how incredibly talented they both were. From the perspective of their IQ, both were geniuses. They were both brilliantly intelligent and artistically talented. Yet, they left nothing behind but a mixed bag of emotions. Neither Pat nor my father received a proper funeral. My father had no one in his life. Pat had purposely estranged himself from everyone beyond his immediate family. When they passed away, they disappeared. No one but me—and, in Pat's case, my sisters—mourned their deaths. They drifted away like dust in the wind.

As I reflected on the way Pat and my father left the world, I realized that I didn't want the same fate. I wanted to leave my mark on this world. I understood that the positive impact I have on the world, and the people around me, will live on when I'm gone. At that moment, I knew, with great certainty, that when my time comes to go, everyone who has known me, worked with me, or otherwise been part of my life will be able to say that Chris Duffin was a part of this world, and that the world is a better place because of it. That message struck home in that moment and has stayed with me ever since, impacting my goals, my approach to leadership, and—most importantly—my parenting style.

NEW JOBS AND MORE RESPONSIBILITY

After Pat passed away and I took custody of Amy, I realized that the trip to Mexico wasn't going to happen. Although I had significant savings, I couldn't live in Portland and not work. I would have been bored. I began working with another window and door manufacturer—the same industry in which I had worked in Klamath Falls, although not the same company. The dot-com boom and bust had radically altered my group of friends. When it was at its peak, lots of people with whom I had graduated college had moved to Portland to work in the dot-com industry. When the bubble burst, most of them lost their jobs and moved on to different roles, with different companies, in different states.

That left me with few friends and a desire to make new connections. Through Greg, I met a woman named Lisa who I was attracted to. I had seen her at parties and knew that she worked as a teacher, and that, like me, she enjoyed the outdoors. In fact, we had once spent a day snowboarding together. Outside of that experience, however, we hadn't spent much time together. I called her up, asked her on a date, and we hit it off.

As Lisa and I became closer, my job with the window and door manufacturer was hitting the skids. It was a crazy environment, with an enormous amount of staff turnover. In the short time I worked there, the plant manager and half of the management staff moved on, creating a highly chaotic atmosphere. The glass department, which fed all the other departments in the plant, performed especially poorly. I noticed it was failing, and the company had recently fired the department manager, so I put my hand up and volunteered to run it. I'd already had a substantial positive impact on the department I was running, so I believed I could make a positive difference.

The plant manager thanked me for stepping up and told

me I had sixty days to fix the problems or I would be fired—an interesting way of saying "thank you." I succeeded in turning around the glass department and reshaped the entire glass production process, reducing the total glass inventory by more than 50 percent. With less glass moving around a giant facility, we also reduced safety and delivery issues. Salvaging the glass department had a huge impact on the factory as a whole.

Following this, the plant manager told me that he wanted me to manage the plant on the swing shift, 4 p.m. until midnight. By this time, Lisa and I were in a solid relationship. As a teacher, Lisa worked during the day. If I worked swing shift, our employment patterns would be totally incompatible. I explained this to the plant manager, but he wasn't interested. When I started working at the plant—in different relationship circumstances—I had indicated that I was willing to work swing shift, so he insisted I take the role, claiming that I should be grateful of the promotion. I didn't see it that way, so I found a new job.

I went to work with an automotive company that manufactured off-roading supplies and direct factory gear-train components for the likes of Ford, Kia, and Dodge. With my burgeoning interest in off-roading, it was a fantastic fit for me. Around the same time as I took the role, I remember Lisa and I putting the Jeep on a trailer and making the twenty-hour drive to Moab, Utah, one of the hottest off-roading and mountain-biking destinations in the world, for a week with friends. That cemented our relationship, just as I was joining a company whose products coincided with my interests.

Before long, I found myself running a sixty-million-dollar division in my new workplace. It was the most successful division in the organization, but it had been stagnating for a while and the marketplace was becoming much more competitive. Chinese knock-offs were beginning to flood the market and the quality was beginning to creep up, turning these knock-offs into serious rivals for our products. Before I took over the department, the company's leaders had attempted to instigate changes in the department. Most of the employees had been working there for more than twenty-five years, however, and they were highly resistant to change.

The department was large, consisting of approximately one hundred employees. Although I wanted to initiate physical changes, my first task was to influence the team's culture, so that the existing employees would become open to improvements. That took a lot of one-on-one conversations, with the objective of communicating my vision for the department and winning the buy-in of my new colleagues. We set up small-scale example projects, scored wins, and then invited those who had participated to describe those wins to other members of the team. Gradually, we built momentum.

Fast forward a couple of years and the department was transformed, from beginning to end. Costs were significantly reduced, and I had brought in several million dollars' worth of new equipment. Along the way, we delivered improved performance, reduced safety incidents, and put in place a process so robust that it continues to operate in the same fashion, fifteen years after I left the company.

With its most successful department restored to profitability, the company put me to work on one that was failing. The company leaders fired all the managers associated with this failing department and brought me and a close colleague of mine in to turn it around. At this point, my reputation was so strong that performance spiked before I even made any changes. Employees were so excited and reinvigorated to work with a leader they respected and say goodbye to the overbearing style they were used to that their motivation increased immediately.

The department in question delivered their products with a six-week lead time. When I took over, we were only meeting that standard 50 percent of the time. Overall, we were eight to twelve weeks behind schedule. By the time I left, we were committing to deliver within between one day and a week, and we met that significantly higher standard at least 75 percent of the time.

Sometimes work was boring or highly demanding. For example, at the automotive supply company, I had ninety direct reports. Imagine sitting down and writing ninety annual reviews, each one three to four pages long. It could take months. Nonetheless, I did it. I felt that I was receiving an education on how to run successful businesses, and I was getting paid at the same time. I knew that, in time, I wanted to run my own business, but I also knew that striking out on my own too early would be costly and slow. Therefore, I looked at every challenge as an opportunity to grow the skills I would one day employ in my own business.

When I finished my reviews, the leadership rated them higher than any other manager's in the entire six-hundred-person company. The HR department requested that I work with them, training other managers on the principles of writing good reviews. That led to me getting involved in a number of other coaching and disciplinary scenarios, as I became known as someone who could get the best out of employees and resolve performance issues. I sat in while they met underperforming employees and acted as a resource, coaching them on how to handle tricky situations more productively.

I knew that I wanted to take every possible opportunity

to learn and master new skills. I see a lot of people half-ass whatever task they put their mind to, often because they think it's not cool to make a lot of effort. My view is that we learn only by applying ourselves fully to the task at hand. Time and again, I dove into challenging situations and came out the other end enriched, with a fresh understanding of my own capabilities.

GOODBYE PAINTBALLING, HELLO COMPETITIVE LIFTING

Before I moved from Klamath Falls to Portland, paintballing was my primary hobby. After the move, I went out and took part in a few games, but the fire was gone. My paintballing friends lived halfway across the state and hanging out with them was the most satisfying part of playing.

I still owned my paintball business in Klamath Falls, however. I started selling off the equipment and simultaneously purchased a commuter vehicle. My Jeep—so associated with my paintballing days—seemed bound for retirement. That is until I discovered that there was a great trail system on the coastal mountain range outside Portland, approximately forty-five minutes from home. Although my schedule was packed, I tried to set aside some time on the weekends to do things I enjoyed. Part of that involved sinking some of the funds I raised through selling my paintballing business into the modification of my Jeep. It was no longer a street vehicle, so I was free to concentrate mainly on performance.

As I focused on building and customizing my Jeep, the focus of my training shifted. I was used to training purely because I liked the challenge. I didn't ask myself whether training would make me *look* better. I only asked myself whether it would make me stronger. This distinction hit home when I noticed a couple of guys in the gym preparing for a body-building show. They were bigger than me, and they looked better, but I was clearly far stronger, and I did more work. This caused me to reflect on where the differences arose from, and to wonder whether I had the strength to compete in a bench press and deadlift meet. I decided to find out.

Although I was entering a competition for the first time, I had about a decade's experience of training, factoring in the two years I took off while I was drinking heavily. Initially, I thought I'd enter as a one-off. I wanted to experience something new and to say that I had competed. I found a bench press and deadlift competition that took place six weeks later, so I signed up. This was the late nineties, when training information was much harder to come by than it is today. I got most of my ideas from bodybuilding magazines and books, which ignored numerous fundamentals. As a result, I didn't even know what a deadlift was. I read the rules, thought I understood, and technically what I performed in that competition qualified as a deadlift. My form and the quality of my movement, however, were poor, verging on tragic.

What I hadn't anticipated was loving competitive lifting so much. By the end of my first day's competition, I knew I would be part of this world for the rest of my life. I qualified for the World Championships of the federation in which I was competing, to take place in Nevada later the same year, and I decided instantly that I would go and take part. This shift gave my training a new focus. Instead of walking into the gym to train purely for the sake of training, I trained with an eye on upcoming bench press and deadlift meets. Later, I switched to full powerlifting, which includes the squat.

In tandem with my substantial work commitments and custom vehicle design and fabrication, training and competing became a central cornerstone of my life. I set up a mini fabrication shop at home, and before long it occurred to me that I needed to do something similar for my body. I was traveling to use a public gym yet providing a lot of my own equipment. I took specialty bars and implements with me that weighed hundreds of pounds and required a heavy bag with wheels to transport. Every time I arrived at the gym, it took me twenty minutes to bring my equipment inside. Essentially, I was bringing my own gym *to* the public gym. It was obvious

I needed to save myself a lot of time and effort and set up my own.

One of my training buddies and I began to custom build a home gym. We fabricated our first squat rack and I said, "This is the first piece of what will one day be a massive, successful gym." Anyone looking in from the outside would probably have been skeptical, but I had a vision in my head of what I could build. The squat rack was only the first step in that direction.

THE RETURN OF MY MOM, AND A DARK FIGURE FROM OUR PAST

While I was raising Amy, my mom began to reappear and become part of my life again. She had moved from Montana back to eastern Oregon, and she was living in a small community named Burns, where she worked at a branch of McDonald's. At first, her contact with the rest of the family was understandably limited. My sisters were resentful that she had abandoned them. While I was comfortable raising them, I was angry and disappointed that she had put them in such a difficult position. Over time, however, my sisters began to reach out more to my mom, arranging meetings and moving toward forgiveness. I felt that the issue was between them, so when my sisters forgave, I followed suit.

She later moved to Mitchell, Oregon, where she lived

with a miner named Leonard Kopinski, also known as Kop. Kop was quite a bit older than my mom and his wife had passed away not long before. My mom took care of him and initially established a business partnership with him. He owned a mine, but he was unable to run it effectively. She took on the responsibility for doing this and they became partners. Over the years, their relationship grew. Eventually they married and she cared for him until his passing.

Leonard was something of a folk legend in eastern Oregon. He walked around with his .44 strapped to his hip, confronting law enforcement officers and wading headfirst into land disputes. He had been a fixture in the local newspapers for decades, reaching back as far as the 1960s or 1970s.

Due to his involvement with land issues and his outspoken nature, Kop had a direct line to his state senator, a highly unusual privilege for a private individual. On one occasion, when I visited Mitchell to see my mom, she told me she had run into the sheriff who arrested her for possession of marijuana, and who had subsequently taken me and my siblings into custody. He had served twenty years in prison for his part in attempting to traffic my sisters. Although she hadn't seen him for over two decades, my mom recognized him immediately. When he realized my mom lived in the same town, he began stalking her.

He drove past her house, extremely slowly. If he saw her at the window, he formed his fingers into the shape of a gun, using his thumb as the hammer, and pretended to shoot at her.

My mom decided that she needed to leave town, so she left her job, packed up her things, and drove away. Before long, she noticed that she was being followed by an associate of the former sheriff. An hour or two out of town, the same car was behind her, keeping its distance. The roads in eastern Oregon are quiet and there wasn't a lot of passing traffic, so it was clear that the driver was traversing the same route as my mom. On reaching a fork in the road, she pulled off the road, exited her vehicle, and pulled out her rifle.

On such a desolate road, in the middle of the desert, there was no telling when someone else might show up. She was completely alone. Moreover, visibility was exceptionally high. Anyone approaching would be visible from miles away. My mom crossed the road to the opposite side, set up her rifle, and stood by the side of the road, waiting for her pursuer. When he came close to her position, he saw her, pulled his truck off the road, and sat there, waiting.

My mom had him at gunpoint, but she didn't know what to do. She told me later that although she never wanted to kill someone, she wasn't sure what she would do if he got out of the car. She told herself she could run into the desert, where it would be nearly impossible for him to find her. Nonetheless, she was known as a wild, self-sufficient, and extremely stubborn woman. There was a possibility in her mind—and probably in her pursuer's mind too—that she might kill him if she felt she needed to.

Eventually, he gunned his truck, made a U-turn in the road, and drove back the way he had come. She jumped into her truck, waited until he was totally out of sight, and drove to Mitchell to meet with Kop.

While she was living with Kop in Mitchell for a couple of months, my mom had an eerie experience. She heard a knock on the door and opened it to see a couple of hunters standing outside. They told her they were lost and asked to use her phone. My mom, ever hospitable, agreed to let them use her phone, but was highly skeptical of their story. She suspected they were connected to the man who had been stalking her in Burns. To convey her distrust, and the fact that she was armed, she pulled out a gun, sat down, and dropped her gun on her lap. Kop was also in the house and registered her response.

She explained the situation and, before long, the police showed up at the former sheriff's home in Burns. The most likely reason for this is that Kop pulled some strings, perhaps by calling his senator, and persuaded the police to search my mom's stalker's home, although I don't know this for certain. The police told the former sheriff that they wanted to search his property because they suspected he was complicit in poaching. Instead, they found the remains of four women he had killed and buried on the grounds of his property.

It turned out that, not only was my mom's stalker heavily involved in human trafficking, he was also a serial killer. In 1985, when my mom sent me running down the street to make sure there were witnesses present as he took her into custody, it's very possible that her request saved her life.

THE AMERICAN DREAM, BUT WAS IT *MY* DREAM?

Home has always meant a lot to me. I want to know that the place where I live is beautiful and that it belongs to me. I want the freedom to customize my living space. When I've found myself living in a rented duplex or a shared apartment, I've noticed that I feel unsuccessful. Perhaps I feel an echo of the transitory life I lived with my parents when I was a child. While I was working at the automotive supply company, I wasted no time in buying a home in Portland, where I lived with my girlfriend and Amy. Amy stayed with us until well into her nineteenth year, a little longer than her two older siblings. Fortunately, Lisa was very supportive of the process, guiding Amy as she found her direction in life and never attempting to push her out before she was ready. The large size of the house eased that pressure, too. Amy wound up making snowboarding and the mountains a cornerstone of her life. To this day, she, her husband, and her children work year-round for a ski resort in Oregon. Lisa was the one who bought Amy her first snowboard.

Me, my sisters, and my youngest nephew in my back yard on the day I married Lisa. You can see the pride in my face at the people they have become.

When Amy moved out, Lisa and I decided that we wanted to marry. In conventional terms, I had achieved the

American Dream. I was successful in my working life, I owned my own house, complete with a white picket fence, and I was getting married. It was my vision of success at the time, and I made it happen. I felt that, by becoming a normal, productive member of society, I'd proved something to anyone who thought I would never amount to anything. During this period, I was also dialing back the off-roading and focusing primarily on my career and marriage.

LESSON: CONSCIOUS SELF-REINVENTION

Following my move to Portland, I fully reinvented myself, taking on new professional challenges, leaving behind my excessive drinking, and getting married. It would be true to say that I wasn't fully aware of my authentic self. My reinvention was based on my beliefs about who I *should* be, rather than on my authentic identity. Nonetheless, I was able to separate myself from negative aspects of my identity, build a strong foundation in my life, and become highly successful—at least, based on my definition of success at that time.

Anyone can do the same. You can do the same. The only question is whether you're willing to make the hard decisions that will move you forward. You may need to draw a line between yourself and some aspects of your current life. For me, those hard decisions required me to cut ties with a number of friends and family members. I deepened my self-discipline, cutting down on play time and pouring my energy into training and studying for an MBA. It's easy to fall into day-to-day habits. The question is whether those habits are creating the foundation of the life you want for yourself.

During almost the entire time period described in this chapter, I had no television in my house. In fact, the same is true when I lived in Klamath Falls. It was only when I got married that my wife and I purchased a TV and occasionally set aside time to watch movies together. Television is a perfect example of a device that feeds on boredom, filling the holes with entertainment while simultaneously preventing people from taking action to improve their lives. When you stop distracting yourself, you'll be amazed at the impact you can have, not only on your own life, but also on the lives of others.

I look back now on the time described in this chapter and I realize that the actions I took had a positive influence on the lives of many people. For example, I showed my sisters how to take responsibility for themselves, providing them with a supportive environment and expecting them to meet high standards of behavior. Without this platform, I think it's unlikely that my sisters would be living the healthy, productive lives they live today. They would have followed in the footsteps of Pat, John, Stoney, or Mark. I didn't do the work *for* them, however. I insisted that they do the heavy lifting.

When I worked at the automotive supply company, it was intimidating to be charged with the responsibility of reconfiguring their most successful department. It was the largest division of any company I'd ever led, with huge downside potential. If my initiatives had failed, the company would have lost a significant albeit depreciating asset. Although not everything I did was perfect, my work made a significant impact on both my colleagues and the company as a whole. Even today, I'm still in touch with people who worked under me at that time.

If you want to reinvent yourself, put in the work and master the skills you need to be successful. You may not even know which skills will be useful to you down the line, and in what context. If it feels like the right move, jump in anyway. It's the only way to learn.

COMING BACK TO CRAZY

After five years with the automotive supply company, I found myself complaining about work a lot. I complained to my wife. I complained to my best friend, Ben. I wasn't frustrated because work was too tough. Quite the opposite. I was bored out of my mind. With no new divisions to turn around, day-to-day maintenance wasn't providing me with the stimulation I needed. I had created a stable life. The life I thought I wanted. A stable job. A stable marriage. And I was bored senseless.

My only outlet for other aspects of my personality was my lifting, competing, and off-road fabrication projects. I'd built my home gym up to the point where I hosted at least twenty people each day. I trained each day and it provided me with a little relief, but not enough to prevent me from feeling that I needed to forge a new path for myself.

I started applying for different jobs internally, in the hope of finding a role that would challenge me. I applied for positions in product development, and also in marketing, neither of which I got. Although I was respected within the company, I was known as the manufacturing guy. When I attempted to broaden my horizons, I was told that I didn't have enough relevant expertise to qualify for the positions I wanted. I argued that, as someone who used the company's products, I was in a great position to understand our consumers, but my protests fell on deaf ears. After punting ideas back and forth for a while, it became apparent that there was little chance for further development in the automotive supply company, so I decided to leave.

I began talking to recruiters about roles around Portland, partly for my own entertainment. One company, an aerospace manufacturing company, reached out to me about a plant manager role. When I interviewed, I spoke to a representative of an investment firm involved with the company. I also spoke to the company's British owner, who seemed highly eccentric. He told me that he wanted me to come in and perfect the plant in Portland, then move on to opening multiple plants around the United States, each one supporting a location where Boeing manufactures airplanes. In addition to all of that, he owned a software firm with which he wanted me to get involved with as well.

It all sounded wild and exciting. Although I didn't understand exactly what was behind the owner's enthusiasm, I could tell that there was something unusual afoot. There were a lot of moving pieces and a lot of challenges. I could stick with my secure job, in an industry connected with my hobby, or I could go out on a limb and take a partially defined role in an aerospace manufacturing company, working under a weird boss. Without much hesitation, I chose the latter.

CHAPTER EIGHT

TRANSFORMATION

2008–2015 (AGE THIRTY-ONE TO THIRTY-EIGHT), PORTLAND, OREGON

It was a Saturday morning in Portland. A little overcast, but I didn't mind. I had plans. Summer was almost over, and fall was fast approaching. The infamous Pacific Northwest rainy season could kick in at any time, so I knew I needed to wrap up my outdoor projects for the year.

Following a light breakfast, I stood in the garden of the property Lisa and I had bought together several years earlier. My objective for the day was to fix several sections of the fence and extend it across the front of the property.

I had two main reasons for the project. The first was to protect the young family we planned to grow. The second was to keep dogs inside. We had lots of friends with dogs, and when they came over there was nowhere for them to run around safely. I decided it was time to change that.

Once I have a project in mind, I like to get started as quickly as I can, and I hate to stop halfway through. This fence-building endeavor was no exception. I had bought all the lumber the day before, and it was sitting on my truck, along with the concrete I needed to set the posts. I was determined to get through all the work in a day.

My first task was to dig post holes. I had borrowed a gasoline-powered, post-hole digger from a friend in the hope that it would speed up the process. Unfortunately, the Portland area used to be a river bed. The soil looks normal on the surface, but just below ground are large, round stones. The post-hole digger wasn't a lot of help. I ended up using a crowbar and my hands to remove the stones manually.

The day rolled on and I refused to take a break. I didn't even want to stop even for five or ten minutes to grab a snack or drink some water. All I wanted was to finish the project. Lisa usually took it upon herself to watch me when I started on a project and force me to stop before I exhausted myself. On this particular Saturday, she was out of the house, so she wasn't there to make sure I took care of myself. Without her direction, I kept pushing myself.

Around twelve hours in, I was close to finishing the fence. That's when the skies opened and the rain began to pour down. Until then, the overcast weather had kept me cool. In comparison with working in the summer, it was relatively pleasant. I was sweating without overheating. Working in the pouring rain was a different story.

I could have called it a day and come back in the morning. But I was determined to finish the task I'd set for myself. I still had dirt to move, rocks to dig out of post holes, and lumber to carry from the truck. The finish line was in sight. I wasn't about to give up.

In an effort to get through the rest of the work, I started running. I was pushing a wheelbarrow full of wood, rocks, and dirt, running as fast as I could across my garden, trying to finish building the fence. I sprinted with a full wheelbarrow in the pouring rain, stopping every thirty seconds or so to forcefully catch my breath. I was putting the same intensity of effort required by a powerlifting competition into building a fence. Drenched to the core and exhausted, I started to dry heave. It was so intense that it stopped me in my tracks.

Even then, I refused to back down. In between dry heaves, I finished the project and wandered inside, about the time my wife returned home. By this point, I had been working outside for around twelve or fourteen hours. I was shivering from the cold and close to collapsing from the fatigue. My wife took one look at me and started laying into me for pushing myself so hard.

She told me I had to stop pushing myself beyond my limits. That I needed to think about what I needed to do to stay healthy, without the need for her to babysit me. That I needed to take breaks for food and water *before* I made myself sick.

I had to admit she had a point. I approached almost everything in life with the same gung-ho attitude, and it wasn't serving me well. The whole winter, I would go from one cold to the next because I was so drained, and I never gave myself a chance to recover. I was entering my mid-thirties, working an executive-level job, training, and starting a second business on the side. I was also a new parent.

I sat in the kitchen, trying to get some fast-acting food into my body, and I gave my wife's words serious consideration. "She's right," I thought. "I can't keep burning the candle at both ends during the week, then come home and do the same on the weekend." I realized it wasn't sustainable and I couldn't continue running at the same pace.

THEME: TRANSFORMATION

In this chapter, you'll read stories about how I put in the work required to turn my vision into reality, on a large scale. As my focus grew laser sharp, both the impact and the consequences of my actions were amplified. As Winston Churchill once said, "the price of greatness is responsibility." As I zeroed in on my true path, I felt the weight of both my successes and my failures deep in my bones.

You'll read stories of painful change, heartbreak, drama, and despair. Equally, you'll encounter stories of deep purpose, perseverance, and victory, of which I am immensely proud. A thin line separates the man who thinks he's perfect and the man who recognizes both his flaws and his achievements. I've made plenty of mistakes in my time, but I've also learned tremendous lessons from those mistakes. You will hear me speak boldly of my accomplishments because I know who I am, and what my purpose is.

Together, these changes cohere into a narrative of intentional **transformation**. Change has been a common thread throughout this book. In this chapter, you will see me take even greater ownership of the changes I chose to create, building on those foundations and experiencing profound victories and defeats in my personal, professional, and competitive life.

As we enter the last quarter of this book, I hope to challenge you to live powerfully and do the hard things that are necessary to build the legacy you will leave, brick by brick and day by day. I will share the psychological tools that I've used and refined during my life and push you to take the practical steps necessary to attain true transformation.

TURNING AROUND AND SELLING A FAILING COMPANY

I left the automotive supply company where I had worked for five years around the time my first child was born. I handed in my two weeks' notice, spent a couple of weeks at home with my wife and son, and then returned to work and a brand-new challenge. My new role was with an aerospace company that supplied critical components directly to Boeing. I was hired as director of operations. My time with the company was an incredibly challenging, yet incredibly rewarding period of my career. I was looking for relief from boredom, and I got it in spades.

Due to the essential nature of the components we supplied, any delivery hiccup longer than a couple of days would lead to disruption in the production chain and a delay in the production of 737s. These airplanes sell for between sixty and eighty million dollars, so failing to meet expectations was a serious matter. When I was hired, the company's owner told me that the firm was performing at an exceptionally high level and that the supply mechanism needed a few tweaks before we could move on to building multiple plants around the country, supporting Boeing operations nationwide.

Within my first couple of weeks in the job, however, it became clear that he had lied to my face. The company was losing money. It was also underperforming—both in terms of quality and in terms of timely delivery—and was in danger of losing its contract with Boeing. If that happened, the organization would go bankrupt and every employee would lose their job. I quickly realized that the owner was purposely attempting to drive the firm into bankruptcy so that he could write off the debt he had accumulated, walk away, and start another business. He was a very unethical individual.

He was also a terrible manager, who directed me to do things I couldn't possibly agree to. Once, he told me to ask everyone in the company to name someone whose job they could do. He wanted me to fire everyone who was named, transferring their responsibilities to the person who named them and doubling the salary of the remaining employee. Then, after six months, he wanted me to reduce the increased salaries back to their original level, in the process halving the size of both the workforce and the company's wage bill.

Even more seriously, his interactions with Boeing were totally counterproductive. By the time I started with the company, we were on probation, meaning that they could decide to terminate our contract at any time. I set up meetings with senior members of staff at Boeing and laid out a plan to improve the situation. They told me that, while they recognized that I was smart and they liked my plan, they had seen the owner sabotage the company's progress time and time again, and then fire the person responsible for boosting productivity and reliability. Understandably, the people I spoke to at Boeing doubted I would be able to implement my plans with him in charge.

Fortunately, I had a plan and was able to turn the tables on him. I detailed the owner's interactions with Boeing in a letter issued both to the investment firm with a stake in the company and to the board of directors. The owner was quickly removed from the board and fired from his own company. Without him creating problems, I spent the next four years turning the company around and was promoted to become general manager of the plant.

There were enormous problems to address. When I began to get a grip on the situation, we were still losing money, which meant we lost our access to credit. A multimillion-dollar company in the aerospace manufacturing industry is extremely expensive to operate, and we had very limited funds available. One of my first jobs was to ensure that employees were paid on time and payment obligations to suppliers were met.

Over the course of four years, I overhauled the process management side of the business, turning chaos into order and generating metrics that allowed us to measure and improve performance. Additionally, I rehabilitated the company culture so that the process changes we had made could take root and flourish. As a result, our performance increased by leaps and bounds. We went from delivering components on time 75 percent of the time to achieving that feat upwards of 99.8 percent of the time. We attained best-in-class status for both the quality of our work and our reliability, placing the company in the world-class bracket.

When I started working at the company, we operated two plants. One in Portland, with over one hundred employees, and a smaller facility in Seattle, Washington, with about twenty employees. While I was able to create tremendous change in Portland, the process improvements had less impact in Seattle. After three years, I made the decision to shut down the Seattle operation. We consolidated the two facilities, moving all the equipment down from Seattle to Portland and giving any employees who wanted to remain with the company the opportunity to relocate.

Financially, we moved from losing millions of dollars per

year to making profits to the tune of millions of dollars per year. Unfortunately, the departed owner's financial mismanagement had consequences even after he was removed from the company. About three years into my tenure, we were seeking to renew and renegotiate our contracts with Boeing. By this time, we were the best supplier in the world of our type, which you might think would have put us in an iron-clad negotiating position. The substantial debt remaining from the company's years of failure, however, weakened our hand and ultimately meant that Boeing's finance team wouldn't renew our contract. This forced the sale of the company.

I put together a presentation, set up meetings with our suppliers and with potential buyers, and started working on a management buyout. The plan was for me and the rest of our senior team—there were four of us in total—to become part owners of the company. At the last moment, a finance company that had invested significantly in the company changed hands, and the new owners chose to divest from the manufacturing sector. They held the board positions, so when they walked away, the original owner returned to the company.

As you can imagine, the owner was extremely unhappy with me. I had tactically engineered his removal from the company. I sent a letter to both Boeing and the company's creditors, explaining that he was ignoring his fiduciary responsibilities in an effort to deliberately bankrupt the organization. In this letter, I told Boeing and the bank that if they didn't help us sell the company, the management team would walk away, leaving it vulnerable to the owner's depredations. Angry though he was, however, the owner couldn't fire me. My profile in the organization had risen too high.

Boeing decided to accelerate the process, by bringing in an outside firm to determine whether the company should be sold or liquidated, and to follow through quickly on that decision. Boeing hired a high-powered New York firm, with whose representatives I and the rest of the management team met. Their first day on the job, one of them pulled up the letter I had sent explaining that the owner was neglecting his fiduciary responsibilities. He read through it, looked right at me, and said, "We have a serious issue here." The implication was that he suspected I was a major root of the problems within the company and that he would need to deal with me. With a few days of research, however, the representatives of the firm concluded that I was telling them the truth. Their biggest task was to keep the owner out of the process while they prepared the sale of the company.

The New York firm decided to auction off the company. With all the groundwork I had done to interest potential buyers, there were twelve bidders. I had spoken to eleven of them and agreed to terms for a management buyout. The twelfth won the auction. The day the organization's new owners took possession, I handed in my notice and moved on. Over the years, I had earned the owners of various companies millions of dollars, in exchange for a good salary. While there was a time when that felt right for me, I had reached a point where I was no longer interested in simply having a job. I wanted an ownership stake in whatever I did next.

I discussed the situation with the aerospace manufacturing company's new owners, and they weren't interested in offering me and the rest of the executive team a management buyout. They were a large, private, international company. They offered to keep me on in an excellent position, with lots of opportunity for career growth, and I turned them down. Nonetheless, their purchase of the firm was a win, because it left with me a sense of completion. I knew my work was done. I had taken the company from failure to success and, in the process, secured the future employment of everyone who worked there. I also spearheaded a shift in the environment from a place driven by stress and fear to one in which people felt good about their roles and knew they were doing the right thing. The employees were exceptionally grateful, and I still talk to some of them today.

Some even work for me.

MY CAREER IN PROFESSIONAL LIFTING

Throughout my time with the aerospace company, while my career was a huge focus, I also focused a lot on powerlifting. I knew that I could be more successful in either discipline if I was willing to drop the other, but I preferred to keep two strings to my bow. It was a subject that often arose in job interviews, as anyone who looks at me can tell that I lift. I always chose to be completely open about my love of strength, explaining that—barring a major tragedy—I would be out the door Mondays and Wednesdays by 4:30 p.m., and that I was not available to work Saturdays.

A lot of my executive peers worked ten- or twelve-hour days, six days per week. I refused to do that, explaining that my results spoke for themselves. Occasionally it was an issue at first, but once people saw what I delivered, they accepted my position. My career may have suffered somewhat because I protected both my lifting and my relationships with my family, but it was worth it to me. As a result, my lifting took off. Many years ago, I realized the importance of a strong methodology. This applies to other areas of life as much as it applies to lifting. To succeed, you need the right equipment, the right methods, and the right people around you.

For me, connecting with Rudy was a big piece of the puzzle. Nowadays, Rudy is my business partner. When we met, he was the only other person I knew who combined success in business with a dedicated lifting schedule. I was rotating through training partners at my home gym and became frustrated by the space restrictions. Shortly after we met, Rudy and I decided to open a gym. We leased a modest four-thousand-square-foot space and moved all my home gym equipment into it. I had so much stuff that it was enough to completely fill the new space. We named our new venture Elite Performance Center (EPC). Later, we renamed it Kabuki Strength, and it would become much more than just a gym.

EPC became ground zero for some incredible feats of strength. From 2008, I was consistently ranked number one in the world at one discipline or another: the squat, deadlift, or full powerlifting. I set several all-time world records. For example, in the 220-pound weight class, I set a squat world record of 860 pounds, which I later bumped to 881 pounds. At that point, I was the heaviest person in history ever to squat four times his own body weight.

As these feats became common knowledge, I became a celebrity in the lifting world. I showed up at events and people wanted autographs and pictures. For a kid who had spent most of his childhood living hand to mouth in the wilderness of California and Oregon, this was a strange experience. Although I received a bit of attention when the *Bend Bulletin* published my story, this was on another level.

THE INTENSE CONSEQUENCES OF CUTTING WEIGHT

During my peak lifting years, I tended to push myself hard. Sometimes too hard. In 2015, I flew to Australia to take part in the World Championships. Following a twenty-hour flight, I was preparing to cut weight so that I could compete in the 220-pound weight class. This was a process I had undertaken many times previously, but each subsequent time I had allowed my weight to increase more and more before commencing the cut. I found myself cutting twenty pounds in a day, then twenty-two, then twenty-five. When I arrived in Australia, I was thirty-nine pounds overweight. I had approximately twenty-four hours to cut thirty-nine pounds, then another twenty-four hours following the weigh-in to bring my weight back up as high as possible. Cutting over 15 percent of my body weight in twenty-four hours was an extreme task by anyone's standards.

To put this into perspective, a typical weight cut for competitive purposes is between six and twelve pounds. Elite lifters sometimes drop as much as fifteen or twenty pounds in a day. At this level, it's vital to have a high degree of knowledge in the science of weight manipulation. Cutting such a large amount of weight in such a short time alters the body's electrolyte balance, which can lead to instantaneous death through heart or kidney failure.

Over the course of my lifting career, I found myself

driven to cut more and more weight. When I began, cutting in the region of fifteen to twenty pounds was a process I enjoyed. It stripped away the trappings of my normal life and took me into a zone of pure focus. Most of the athletes I competed against were full-time, elite lifters. Lifting was their job, perhaps in conjunction with owning a gym or working as a brand ambassador. My priorities were different, I was working full time as an executive and had hard rules about protecting my family life.

With so much on my mind, cutting weight initially felt like a spiritual experience. In everyday circumstances, my job never left me. I was always thinking about some problem I was looking to solve or a meeting I needed to schedule. During and after a weight cut, there was none of that noise. While in the midst of the weight cut process, I experienced powerful epiphanies about my priorities or my future. Afterward, I was 100 percent focused on the upcoming competition. By the time I cut thirty-nine pounds for the meet in Australia, however, I was definitely pushing myself too hard.

At the elite level, the competitive lifting community is small. I already knew many of the people who were there, either in person or via online interactions. I hung out with several other lifters who were known as big weight cutters and we hit the sauna together. Long flights cause water retention, so cutting weight was especially challenging. One by one, the other lifters left the sauna, until I was the only person still in there cutting weight.

Well, not quite the only person. In an illustration of how tightly knit the lifting community can be, a friend of mine stayed with me. Sam Byrd was the squat world record holder in the 220-pound weight class, at 854 pounds, until I surpassed him with 860. He had recently taken a couple of years off competing until he decided to return and take part in the World Championships in Australia. He knew he couldn't beat me, so he was cutting weight to compete at 198 pounds, a weight class below me.

Around midnight, however, Sam realized that he wasn't going to make weight. He got down around 210 pounds, but his body refused to drop any more weight. Instead of quitting, however, Sam stayed with me in the sauna, helping me and encouraging me. If I had failed to make weight for the 220-pound class, that would have been to his advantage. He could have beaten anyone else in that division. Simultaneously, spending time in the sauna when he no longer had any hope of dropping below 198 pounds put unnecessary strain on his body, hurting his performance and further reducing the chances of beating me. Yet he did it anyway. In addition to Sam, Andrei Miclea, a friend of mine who flew down to film the meet, was also with us.

Around 2 a.m., the process of cutting weight became excruciatingly difficult. Sam was taking a nap break and I was on my own, with Andrei checking every few minutes to make sure I was okay. I knew I still had five more hours of sauna time before I dipped below 220 pounds, and those five hours seemed like an eternity. I had my sauna suit on, and it was time for my next shift, but I couldn't bring myself to move. My face was white, and I burst into tears. Andrei looked at me and asked what was wrong. I explained that I was terrified of stepping foot in the sauna again, knowing that I had another five hours of extreme heat ahead of me. I was so terrified of the heat and the pain that I began to weep.

Me during my intense weight cut in Australia, as I struggled to shed 15 percent of my body weight in twenty-four hours.

At this level of intensity, cutting weight is an intensely dangerous practice. After each session in the sauna, I walked around the pool with Sam to maintain my body temperature and prevent myself from going into shock. I kept a nurse or a nurse's assistant on hand during sauna sessions, a phone call away, in case I needed help from a medical professional. I even inserted IV catheters into my arms. I learned to do this myself as an insurance policy. During weight cutting the body becomes very dehydrated, resulting in decreased systemic blood flow. If I collapsed and my veins had shrunk too far, it could have been difficult for my nurse to insert an IV and rehydrate me with fluids. Had I arrived with IVs pre-fitted, however, the process would have been much simpler and faster. Scary as this sounds, it's simply good preparation when undertaking such an extreme activity.

I kept pushing through and at about 6 a.m., I knew I was close to my goal. At this point, however, I lost my hearing. I was already slurring my speech, and suddenly I was also unable to hear. Over the next couple of hours, it returned weakly, although I was still struggling to hear properly. Weigh-ins were due to take place at 9 a.m., approximately forty-five minutes' drive from the sauna. At 7:30 a.m., my team told me I was half a pound overweight and I only needed one more session. Through the fog of my impaired mind, I knew they were mistaken. I needed at least two more twenty-minute sessions to drop the final half-pound.

I looked at them, defeated, and said I'd give it ten more minutes. I knew it wouldn't be enough, but I had given up. I was going to come in overweight and, at that point, I no longer cared. As I sat in the sauna, however, a change came over me. "No," I thought. "I'm not giving up. I'm Chris Duffin. I can do anything. I've got this." I sat in the sauna for about thirty-five minutes, without a break. My teammates were looking at me through the window, knocking on the door, and checking whether I wanted to come out. I kept signaling that I wanted them to stay outside, because if they opened the door, heat would escape. When I felt I had done enough, I signaled to them to come and get me. They entered the sauna, picked me up, and carried me to the car. I couldn't walk or talk. They drove me to weigh-ins, where I was just able to stand long enough to step on the scales. I successfully made weight. The day of a powerlifting competition, I should have been the strongest I had ever been, but only twenty-four hours prior, I was weaker than I had been for years.

With the long flight and the intense weight cut, I had been awake for almost three days. All I wanted to do was sleep. Unfortunately, that wasn't an option. I needed to eat constantly to recover my strength, take in IV fluids, and do some light gym work to increase blood flow and shuttle the carbohydrates and liquids I was taking in to my muscles. By the time I went to bed at around 11 p.m. that night, I had regained the entire thirty-nine pounds. The next morning, I woke up and competed.

Perhaps due to the fact that Australia is a long flight from almost everywhere else in the world, causing competitors to retain a little more water than usual, I was the only lifter to successfully pull off a major weight cut for the meet in Australia. As a brief primer, in competitive powerlifting each participant has three attempts at each discipline: squat, deadlift, and bench press. Successful completion of a specific weight enables a competitor to move on to a higher weight, with final weights added up to reach a final total. Anyone who fails three times at any discipline without registering a successful lift is disqualified from the competition. I won my class, squatting 840 pounds and registering a 2,060-pound total. In fact, I squatted more than anyone in the 242-pound weight class. The only person in the competition who squatted more was the world record holder in the 275-pound class.

While I succeeded in cutting weight for the competition in Australia, I believe I came within half an hour of death. I took a lot of precautions, I monitored my electrolyte levels, and I knew exactly what I was doing. I believe it was only my total dedication to the process that kept me alive. For this reason, I rarely talk or write about cutting weight, and I refuse to publish the details of my methods. I don't want anyone attempting to emulate me.

Dropping twenty pounds can prove fatal. Anything beyond twenty pounds is incredibly dangerous. I cut thirty-nine pounds. Looking back, I think I only achieved that because I was extraordinarily driven, because I had been lifting for a long time, and because I increased the amount I was cutting in small increments per meet. Even so, I don't think it is a good strategy. I succeeded *despite* my extreme weight cutting, not because of it. I wish I hadn't done it and I think I could have been substantially more competitive if I'd chosen a different path.

To give you an example of the severe impact cutting so much weight has, here's a story from a local competition. My business partner, Rudy, and I shared an office at the gym we had opened together. The night before weigh-ins, I left work, cut more than thirty-five pounds to make weight, and walked back into the office the following morning. I stood next to Rudy in the office; he told me that weigh-ins didn't start for half an hour and asked why I was in his office. The weight cut had caused my face to look so ghostly and depleted that he didn't recognize me and thought I was one of the lifters waiting to weigh in. This is a business partner and friend who saw me almost every day. I had to tell him, "Rudy, it's me."

My ghostly face after an intense overnight weight cut. When I stepped into my office, my business partner didn't recognize me.

In addition to cutting weight almost to the point of death, my tendency to push myself beyond my own limits led to several injuries. I ripped the sternal *and* clavicular heads of my left pectoral muscle off the bone where they attach to the arm. They were surgically reattached. While squatting a heavy weight at a meet, I tore my groin, partially detaching it from the bone. I can still hear the sound it made; like a slightly wet newspaper being torn to pieces, except that it was the belly of my muscle ripping apart. I recovered from the physical injury in three to four months. The mental scars took a year and a half to heal. Every time I went down into a squat, I half-expected to hear the same sound.

The catalog of injuries goes on. I detached one of the

heads of my right bicep from the bone, and it has never been reattached. During the course of writing this book, I detached one of my right hamstring muscles (there are three) while attempting to deadlift 880 pounds. One of our core pillars at Kabuki Strength is charity, and I was trying to raise money for a children's cancer research organization. By performing the feat for thirty days in a row. I made it seventeen days. I've had surgery on both of my elbows and have a very limited range of motion in those joints.

Although I don't feel a lot of pain due to the nervous system disorder that allowed me to stay calm when I broke my arm as a child, my lifting and daily life are impacted by the injuries in my elbows. One of the reasons I hate talking on the phone is because it's practically impossible for me to hold a phone up to my ear, so I need to rely on the speakerphone. Sometimes, due to the way I need to position my body to accomplish these tasks, people think my mannerisms when I eat or drink are odd.

CUTTING OUT EVERYTHING NONESSENTIAL

My entire life, I've been all-in. Whatever I commit to, I give it everything I've got. If a friend asked me for a weekend hunting trip, I would buy a whole new tranche of equipment and research the local flora and fauna. Lisa helped me understand this aspect of my personality. She showed me that, although I'm talented and I can achieve what I set my mind to, I need to make decisions about exactly *what* I set my mind to. With a little more discernment, I can accomplish a lot more than I can by tackling every scenario that comes my way.

As a result of this realization, I narrowed my focus enormously during the period covered by this chapter. Anything that fell outside of work, lifting, family, and vehicle fabrication was cut. For example, I hired a groundskeeper to mow my lawn and a cleaner to clean the house. Actions like this helped me to conserve bandwidth for my true priorities.

Despite this shift, I was still pushing myself incredibly hard. My job was a high-risk position, with the possibility that I could lose everything at any moment if a superior decided I wasn't meeting expectations. My lifting was incredibly intense. Although I have accomplished some incredible feats of strength, I think I could have performed a lot better if I had taken a step back and stopped pushing myself to the limit in multiple disciplines at the same time. Lisa challenged me repeatedly, telling me that it was challenging for her and—later—our kids to watch me drive myself so hard. As the injuries mounted, I began to feel that she was right. It was time to dial back the intensity and reduce the risk of damaging myself.

The time had come to retire from competitive lifting. I picked a meet nine months ahead and set myself one final goal: to total 2,200 pounds in the 220-pound weight class, making me the lightest person ever to lift ten times their body weight. This had been a goal of mine for a number of years, but I had never quite achieved it. While I had the strength, cutting weight hampered my performance.

Additionally, rapid weight manipulation sometimes caused my hands to swell—a well-known phenomenon in the powerlifting world—which made it much harder to hold a bar. The process of cutting weight and the goal of realizing maximum strength in competition are directly at odds with each other—cutting weight made me weaker just as competition required me to bring forth my strongest self. As is often the case in life, the pursuit of performance is a matter of balancing extremes. I wanted to give it one more shot and then I would retire, whatever the outcome.

Unfortunately, this was one goal I would never realize. Not only did I fail to meet the 2,200-pound target, I "bombed out," meaning that I didn't complete enough successful lifts to be awarded a powerlifting total. To the outside observer, my performance looked like a disaster. To me, it was confirmation that retiring was the right choice, at the right time.

HARNESSING MY CREATIVITY—SOMETIMES TO EXTREMES

I've always enjoyed making things. It gives me a creative output and the satisfaction of using the things I create. While it's not as high a priority as work, lifting, or family, it's nonetheless important. Fabricating vehicles is an example of this drive. Another example is my approach to gym equipment. After Rudy and I opened what would become Kabuki Strength, I became frustrated by the quality of some of the equipment. It seemed to me that the manufacturers hadn't thought through the ergonomics of the things they were building, meaning they were less effective than they should have been. I started to rebuild existing gear and make new pieces from scratch, before using myself as a guinea pig to test everything out. The quantity grew, to the extent that the gym was soon packed with custom equipment I had created. Meanwhile, I filled the garage space vacated by the closure of my home gym by turning it into a machine shop and using it to fabricate four-wheel-drive vehicles.

I loved building things that would make my family's life better. While this chapter opens with the story of me building a fence, that was a minor project in comparison with adding an entire story to our home. I secured the relevant permits and started the project one spring, when I knew I could expect good weather. Prior to undertaking this huge project, my only experience of home remodeling was the occasional door or window installation, along with a few other small projects. Adding an entire new story was on a different level: I started by cutting the entire roof off my house and disposing of it. As I stood in the middle of the house looking up, there was nothing between me and the sky.

As I had done many times before, I put myself in a difficult spot on the assumption that I would find a way through. If I failed, my house would be without a roof when the rains started in the fall. I reinforced the joists, learned to plumb, did my own electrical work, and brought every element of the newly added floor up to code. The project took me all summer and I finished in the nick of time, just as the first fall rains began. In fact, the first rain arrived before I had finished sealing every part of the new roof, causing some damage to the ceiling on the main floor of the house. When the rain broke, I sealed all the corners with flashing and sealant to repel the rain, then added the siding and the roofing as quickly as I could. Although the construction of the new story was something of a seat-of-the-pants process, it was an incredible space. I added a master bedroom, master bathroom, and a nursery.

SEEING MY LEGACY REFLECTED IN THE EYES OF MY CHILDREN

Two thousand and twelve saw the birth of my daughter. Since I became a parent, I have spent much more time reflecting on my life than I did previously. I wouldn't trade the experiences I've had with anyone; they shaped me and gave me the opportunity to become who I am. Nonetheless, as I watched my children grow and compared their lives with the strange and crazy life I knew at a similar age, I was thankful they wouldn't have to go through a similar childhood to mine. These reflections also gave me the impetus to think again about the life I was building. I had been through another transformation, and yet I still questioned myself. Is this really who I am? Is there more that I want to accomplish in this life? What is it that I truly love doing?

I firmly believe that, while many people spend their time chasing—and sometimes accomplishing—goals, too few of us understand our underlying values. For this reason, we may set goals for ourselves that aren't aligned with our true values and sense of identity. When we do this, even our accomplishments feel foreign. I understood that the element I loved the most about my work was mentoring people, encouraging them, and helping them achieve goals they had never previously imagined possible. I didn't care all that much about airplane parts. I enjoyed working with people, supporting them as they pushed themselves into uncomfortable areas and discovered new capacities in themselves. I realized, too, that I naturally facilitated similar experiences at the gym. I loved coaching people more than I loved lifting. I loved watching a trainee succeed—through overcoming pain, winning a meet, or however else they defined success—more than I loved setting a world record.

I wondered whether I wanted to become some kind of clinician and contemplated going back to school to become a kinesiologist, physical therapist, or chiropractor. I started attending clinical seminars to broaden my knowledge base. At the same time, I was puzzled over the state of my own body. I'd gone years without sustaining injuries, then within a period of a few years I needed multiple surgeries. Whenever I met a surgeon, they focused on the immediate issue and what it would take to correct it. I knew that there was a bigger picture, and that the many injuries I was suffering were interconnected.

In my quest to understand both the field as a whole and my own body, I developed strong relationships with mentors in physical therapy, spine biomechanics, developmental kinesiology, and related disciplines. I attended numerous seminars and continuing education courses. When I understood what the lecturer was teaching, I usually discovered that I could explain it in a different way and often, a few days in, found myself delivering a mini-presentation on some of the material from the course. This journey led me to forge strong friendships with some of the top researchers and clinicians in the world.

The work they were doing fascinated me, but I wanted to

take it to a different place. Most of the clinical data was related to sedentary, nonathletic populations. I wanted to connect the dots and apply their insights outside the clinical realm in a way that anyone could use. This led me to start my own YouTube channel and produce coaching videos on the concepts I was studying as they related to movement under load.

LESSON: TRANSFORMATION

Transformation rarely happens on its own. Typically, it's triggered by some form of stimulus. Sometimes the stimulus is external. To really shape your life, however, you may need to generate your own stimulus. As you've seen in this chapter, I transformed my home environment, building an entire new story onto my home. I transformed my training environment, relocating my home gym to a four-thousand-square-foot facility and opening a commercial gym with Rudy. More than in any previous chapter, however, I also transformed my internal environment, by investigating the intricacies of my own mind and motivations, and by reassessing the way I was approaching my life. This kind of transformation doesn't happen by accident. It only occurs through deliberate effort and self-reflection.

As Shakespeare wrote, "This above all; to thine own self be true." While Shakespeare's conception of truth is not bound by time, it is contingent on a central pillar that is increasingly difficult to attain in today's world—true self-understanding. We live in an individualistic world, where self-expression is supposedly prized, yet the forms that self-expression can take are heavily mediated by social pressures. If we switch on the television or walk past a billboard, we may receive the message that the way to be true to ourselves is to buy a new brand of aftershave or a car. It's a shallow, curated form of individualism.

No one else knows who you *really* are. Nor can they sell you a pill or a consumer good that will magically do the work for you. If you're willing to pursue the path of active transformation, I urge you to seek out an honest understanding of your true self. In Bruce Lee's words, "To become different from what we are, we must have some awareness of what we are."

It's scary to venture into unknown places, either internally or externally. We're creatures of habit, who naturally seek to avoid the pain and difficulty that comes with embracing change. If you want to transform, however, you will need to fight that tendency day in and day out. I've done that by throwing myself into unstable and unpredictable situations, forcing myself to adapt and learn as I find a way through. I tore the roof off my house and put myself in a position where I needed to figure out how to rebuild it before the rainy season began. I took on a job only to discover that the owner was deliberately running the company into the ground, and instead of playing it safe and calling it quits, I decided to take ownership of the situation and do something about it. I choose to take ownership of my circumstances and mold the internal and external world to my will. I choose to leave my mark on this world.

For me, shaping my environment and having a tangible impact on the world is a powerful, deeply satisfying driving force behind my choices. In business, in the weight room, and in every other aspect of my life, I love to walk into a situation and alter it for the better. I love helping people believe in themselves and achieve things they never thought possible. Over the period described in this chapter, I found myself doing this more and more. I supported people to step up and become more than they thought was possible.

This process has an incredible impact in all aspects of a person's life. When we go beyond the bounds of what we thought we could accomplish, we alter our self-perception, becoming more confident in all aspects of life. I've seen situations where a person takes responsibility for a difficult project at work, then decides to go back to school and study for a degree, or to pursue a dream that they always cherished, but never believed they could fulfill.

All meaningful transformation is guided and sustained by

our deepest convictions, whether we are aware of them or not. What do you truly value? Family? Adventure? Financial stability? Whatever it is, you can't measure your success by the values of other people. Do you believe that you'll be happy if you own a mansion and a fancy car? If so, dig a little deeper. What values will those things express?

The fancy car and the house are symptoms of a deeper goal. I'm not here to reshape your morality or tell you what you should value, simply to ask "why?" Financial security and providing for your family are valid motivations behind your life choices. Or maybe you just love cars and houses. Whatever your reasons, however, understand that your decisions are rooted in deeper values, whether or not you are aware of them. The more clearly you understand those values, the more capable you will become of leveraging your efforts in an optimal way. My challenge to you is to dig deeper, and always to ask "why?"

The true goal is meeting the values *behind* your achievements. When you realize this, you can take a step back and choose your path wisely, with full awareness. Start with your values and build goals that are a true extension of who you are; goals that bring deep satisfaction to the soul and leave the world a better place than you found it.

If you're contemplating change in your life, I want you to engage in the practice of Socratic self-examination and give to yourself the attention and effort that is too often wasted on fleeting things. Are you happy with the current state of your life and, if not, why not? What's missing for you? What is it about your life that you find unacceptable right now? Keep asking that question and dive deeper. Do you think that having more money or a better job will take away the itch, or is there something more fundamental you need to express if you're going to be happy with the way you spent your time on this planet? If you're comfortable where you are, that's fine. Not everyone *wants* to drive major change. But if you have a burning desire to leave your mark on this world, you must be painfully honest with yourself. You must look repeatedly for the gaps where you can become a better version of yourself.

You're not the same person as you were ten years ago, or twenty years ago. Throughout our lives we all change and evolve, whether we wish to or not. Only a few, however, make a deliberate choice to actively *seek* change. Transformation comes when we marry the desire for change with a strong sense of purpose and intent, and then we take action. I like to talk about gut-check leadership. If you truly need to make a change, you'll feel it deep in your gut when you are confronted with a dilemma. Your stomach will begin to twist, and you'll know that you can't be right with yourself until you take action.

Existential philosopher Soren Kierkegaard called this

phenomenon the "dizziness of freedom," an inescapable confrontation between the present and future self. Even if you're scared, your gut won't let you escape from the need to jump, to make a change, and to become who you can be. Your gut will tell you what's important. It will also tell you what's *not* important.

If you don't feel a physical reaction in the face of major change, again, ask yourself why. Self-initiated change is an act of self-destruction, a willful aggression of the self. When faced with a potent choice, you *should* feel your heart pounding and your stomach rising toward your throat. If you're apathetic and indifferent, what does that mean? Whenever you feel your gut twist, it's an indication that there's something for you to do: a conversation to have, a project to take on, a decision to make. Heed that signal and run toward it.

LEAVING THE CORPORATE WORLD IN PURSUIT OF PURPOSE

By luck or design, shifts in my work life coordinated with the birth of my children. Leaving the automotive company for the aerospace company coincided with the birth of my first child, Briley. Then, just as my first daughter, Coralie, entered the world, I left the aerospace company and moved to a firm that manufactured hydraulics and custom equipment. I decided to take the job because the owner was intending to build a leadership team that could grow the company to the next level, turning what was a regional firm into one that operated nationally and internationally. His plan was to build a team of highly skilled executives to oversee the transition, then sell the company either to his leadership team or to another buyer with provision for a management buyout.

I played a role fleshing out the team and building the systems required to take the organization to the next level. For example, I led the company through ISO certification—a massive undertaking for a company of this size, especially one with no quality management system in place. It was an important step in ensuring the stability of our internal processes, as well as legitimizing our operation as an international supplier. I promoted an internal manager, Paul, to the role of quality manager, and worked with him to build systems, processes, and a culture of quality in an organization that was in desperate need of those enhancements.

This process usually takes a few years to complete. When auditors review the first iteration, they typically provide feedback in the form of numerous "findings" that require follow-up work to ensure compliance. We completed our work in only nine months, and the audit resulted in zero findings. Throughout my years with this organization, I also undertook massive projects in process development, systems modernization, inventory management, and most importantly, the mentorship of other leaders. I won't bore you with the details of those endeavors, however, except to say that the skills I learned during this phase of my career would serve me well in the massive undertaking that was yet to come.

While I enjoyed the new challenges that came with the role, I was also defining my deeper values in life. When I left the aerospace manufacturing firm, I knew that I wanted an ownership stake in whatever I did next. My role with the hydraulics firm offered that possibility, but it didn't feed my deeper hunger for meaning. I was realizing that my biggest priorities in life are my family and my children, and that I never want them to experience the stresses and strains that constituted my daily life growing up. Additionally, I was still driven by the determination to leave a mark on this world and discovering that one of the most profoundly satisfying ways I can do that is to teach people about strength.

As my children began to grow, it became clear to me that I couldn't sustain my existing pace. Something would have to give. I saw that a career as an executive, combined with running a gym, coaching, competing, and a little hobby time, was not compatible with being a present and engaged father. I was pushing too hard, in too many different directions, just as my wife said. Although I had made a name for myself in the industry and was well compensated, I knew where my heart lay and which priorities I truly valued. Without a speck of doubt, I quit my career and devoted myself to building a legacy.

CHAPTER NINE

LEGACY

2015–2018 (AGE THIRTY-EIGHT TO FORTY-ONE), PORTLAND, OREGON

I wanted to complete my second elbow surgery before I left my job at the hydraulics firm and lost my health insurance. I went in for the procedure on a Monday and, with the medications, I was a little goofy and nauseous. I was knocked out for more than half a day, which was a disorienting experience. I wasn't allowed to go into work or train for several days, so I decided to make the most of my free week.

For some time, I had been considering a second tattoo. The Ouroboros reflected the purposeful reinvention that had become a major theme in my life, and I felt ready to make a statement that demonstrated my commitment to this path. The problem was that the design and placement I had in mind was a large undertaking that would mean approximately forty hours of needle time. A four-hour session is usually considered long, so forty hours of tattooing are typically broken down into ten or more sessions. With breaks for recovery, that amount of work can take as long as a year to complete.

I didn't want to wait that long. I knew I couldn't do anything else for a week so, the day after surgery, I set my alarm, got up in the morning, and took myself to my tattooist for a nine-hour session. We only stopped when my artist was exhausted. I did the same the following day, and the one after, and continued until my tattoo was complete. I figured that if I had to lie around all day, I might as well lie around on a tattoo bench.

My tattoo artist was fantastic. Most artists don't have the stamina to complete nine-hour sessions for several days straight. If they tried, they would succumb to physical or mental fatigue. The work was painful, covering my sternum, ribcage, and armpits, but I wanted to get it done. I had a vision in my head, and I wanted to realize that vision as quickly as possible. Doing nothing for a week would have felt like a total waste of time to me, so I chose to use the time productively. By the end of the week, I had a fresh new tattoo and I was ready to recreate myself once again.

THEME: BUILDING A LEGACY

Everything you've read so far in this book is about a different version of me. I hope you've found the stories I've shared with you both inspirational and instructive, but please understand that they no longer define who I am today. As I continue to reinvent and reshape myself, those past identities feel like old skins, long since shed. Today, I live with deep purpose, molding the world around me in a positive way. I choose to live each day in a deliberate, conscious fashion. If you didn't know a single thing about my past, you could look at who I am and what I'm doing in the world and know that it represents a true image of who I am. I'd like for you to be able to say the same thing for yourself.

The work I do today, the thing that gets me out of bed in the morning and animates my life, is **building the legacy** I wish to leave when I depart this world. It's my way of honoring Pat and my father, who passed away with nothing to their name and almost no one to remember them. In this chapter, you'll read about the process of paring down my identity until I became exceptionally clear about who I am and the extent of my vision. That process also involved cutting ties with some people and situations that no longer represented me accurately. I left a successful career, stopped interacting with some people I had been close to, and removed all obstacles that were holding me back from expressing who I truly am, in business and in life.

You might be surprised at the clarity with which I am able to make difficult choices that alter the course of my life. You may feel that such ruthlessness is unnatural, even robotic, and that life is never black and white. I counter that indecisiveness and apathy are the products of self-ignorance and of a comfortable world that coddles and indulges us. I urge you to consider the consequences of living a life that is not aligned with your true self and your purpose. The fear you feel today is nothing compared to the eternal despair of coming face-to-face with who you could have been and realizing that you failed to answer the call. As Kurt Vonnegut eloquently said, "Of all the words of mice and men, the saddest are, 'it might have been.'"

At times, letting go of people and roles that I once held dear has been extremely painful, as have the challenges of developing a business from scratch and pushing the boundaries of my body's capabilities. That pain is much less excruciating, however, than the pain of continuing to live out of alignment with my true purpose.

While it may initially seem morbid, I invite you to consider the inevitable day when you will lie on your deathbed and meet your mortality head-on. What will you regret not doing? What parts of your life consume your valuable, limited time and energy? Will these things still have meaning to you on the last day of your life? If these questions aren't enough to wake you up, go and spend some time with someone close to you, who is coming to the end of their life. Ask them what they regret and what they would do differently.

Don't leave anything on the table.

EATING MY OWN TAIL

By the time I left my job at the hydraulics company, I knew it was time to get to work and build my purpose in this world—helping people discover their strength in all its forms: physical, mental, emotional, and even spiritual. In short, I knew that I wanted to build an organization that would help people live better through strength. While the intention was clear, I could also see that there were numerous obstacles in my path. I had work to do, stripping away everything that was not essential before I could express the core of my being through work and family life.

The first element that needed to change was my career. I had a lot invested in my professional identity, with multiple advanced degrees and almost twenty years of hard-won professional experience. I was respected and sought after in my field, with an exceptional track record of delivering massive change in a sustainable fashion, with the buy-in of everyone involved. That wasn't an identity I could simply walk away from. I needed to make sure that I was putting in place structures that would remain active for years to come, ensuring that the work I had done would continue and the people whose working lives I impacted would continue to have meaningful and well-paid jobs.

One of the toughest elements of this process, much tougher than putting in place a framework that allowed me to transition to a new working environment, was divorcing Lisa. In previous chapters, I've described the many benefits she brought to my life. I'll always appreciate those qualities and I have only positive words to say about her influence in my life. She's an incredible woman and the mother of my first two children. Ultimately, however, her outlook and mine are very different, and those differences made us incompatible as partners.

I thrive in the midst of change and chaos. I love to be in situations where I'm pushing boundaries and influencing the world. Sustaining that mindset, however, takes a lot of energy. In my home life, I need the support of someone who thinks the same way as I do and feels equally comfortable with change. Lisa preferred a more solid, stable, environment. While that's a perfectly valid approach, it became clear to me that we wanted different things. I wanted to press on and create something new and bold in the world, while she wanted me to slow down and consolidate.

I couldn't fight on two fronts. I couldn't win the battle to establish Kabuki Strength at work, then come home and fight with Lisa for the validity of my vision. While I have no doubt that parting from her was the right decision, it was still extremely painful. Not only was I adapting to the loss of a partner, I felt that I was at risk of putting my children in a difficult, traumatic environment, something I never, ever wanted to do.

As I described in the previous chapter, watching my kids grow helped me to see how bizarre and unconventional my own childhood had been. I was absolutely committed to ensuring that they never experienced the same hardships I did. Yet their mother and I were divorcing. I had seen so many cases of separation or divorce that harmed the children, and I didn't know how badly my own kids would be affected by the experience. That uncertainty brought a lot of stress, anxiety, and depression into my life. I'm not proud of every decision I made during this period. I made some poor choices. Nonetheless, Lisa handled the situation admirably, and we succeeded in creating a lot of continuity for our children as we adapted to co-parenting.

When Lisa and I parted, I felt defeated and believed that it would be almost impossible to find a partner who was aligned with my vision. I assumed that I would spend the rest of my life as a single parent, suffering from loneliness and an unmet need to share affection and love. In the event, I was saved from that fate not by my good looks or killer personality, but through the contagious combination of value, vision, and victory for which I had bled my whole life. Fittingly, it was my sense of purpose that drew my incredible second wife, Jacqueline, into my life.

Jacqueline is a magnificent woman whose heart is perfectly aligned with mine. Her beauty and grace are unsurpassed, matched only by her wisdom and by the fervent love that sustains me through all the craziness of life. Sharing my life with a counterpart like her is a blessing I never expected to find. And I didn't—she found me. The joy, passion, and love we share is an endless source of strength in a life where I accepted the pain and burden of always creating my own strength.

As early as age ten, I understood the power of relationships to support a happy, successful life—or, alternatively, to bring pain and dissatisfaction. When we surround ourselves with like-minded people, we amplify our capacities and get to experience the joys of friendship in the context of purposeful living. The opposite is equally true: those whose presence in our lives doesn't build us up, will drag us down. As I stripped away everything that was holding me back, I also needed to put some distance between certain people I had previously been close to. These were people who I considered friends, mostly because we shared the same interests or hobbies, but whose company didn't lift me up. Some were negative or emotionally draining. Others lacked drive and vision, negatively impacting those around them. In every case, I came to the realization that I needed to prune those relationships from my life if I wished to move forward. Some were long-standing friends, so this was a difficult thing to do.

Most significantly, I found it necessary to cut ties with a man who, over the course of our relationship, had become a public figure in the field of sociology. I won't mention his name here because I don't wish to give the situation additional oxygen. It's not clear to me whether his views had become more extreme over time, or whether he simply grew in confidence as he became more famous. What I do know is that, over time, he began to publicly express perspectives with which I felt extremely uncomfortable. I found myself reading his work and feeling profoundly against the views he espoused. Despite our friendship, his belief system and mine were worlds apart.

I drew strength from my recollection of Pat's decision to estrange himself from his family. At the time, I found it impossible to understand how he could have chosen never to interact with members of his family again. As an adult, I knew how it felt to separate myself from someone based on an insurmountable difference of values. When I found myself cutting ties for difficult, yet necessary, reasons, Pat's stance made a lot more sense to me. Understand that some people are part of your history, but not of your legacy. Letting go is okay.

This multitude of shifts in my personal and professional life brought me face-to-face with the depression that had dogged me for my entire life. I experienced powerful suicidal thoughts and feared that I might become the next in a long line of people on my father's side of the family to leave this world by their own hand. At times, I began to think practically about ending my life. It was a scary time in my life, especially so because I was plagued by the persistent thought that many members of my family had taken their own lives. More seriously, being the methodical person I am, I planned exactly how, where, and when I wanted to do it. The appointed time came and went, and I'm still here. That's all I have to say about that.

To address these issues, I took action and hired a therapist. He worked with me to heal the pain and depression brought about both by my immediate circumstances and by reckoning with my past. A willing and objective listener can do wonders in helping us understand and conquer internal conflict. Vulnerability is only a weakness when it lacks a purpose, and there is no shame in seeking counsel.

I shared some of the stories in this book with him, and

he looked at me, amazed. He told me that he couldn't understand why I wasn't dead, in jail, or addicted to drugs. Everything about my upbringing, he suggested, put me at risk of serious dysfunction in adulthood.

Although this process was incredibly painful, it was absolutely necessary. I needed to free myself from the relationships that held me in stasis before I could move forward and create a new life for myself and those I loved. I had reached a point where anything less than living from a deep sense of purpose was simply unacceptable to me, no matter the cost. Whatever I needed to walk through to manifest my legacy in the world, I would walk through it.

One man who remained in my life throughout this period, and who has been a stable rock of support during turbulence and chaos, is my business partner, Rudy. We became fast friends around the time we launched EPC together, and we have continued to work together ever since. Rudy is not only my business partner, he's also my friend and mentor. He's an incredibly successful businessman who holds multiple powerlifting records, and who continues to shatter perceptions about what is possible. At seventy years old, Rudy can squat nearly 500 pounds, bench press more than 315 pounds, and deadlift almost 550 pounds. He is a living, breathing testimony that age is just a number, and that it's never too late to start cultivating strength. Rudy began to train when he was fifty-five and is breaking world records to this day.

In addition to being highly successful and driven in his own right, Rudy provides the balance that allows me to function as the creative hub of the business we run together. As I've pared down my life, I've handed off the operations side of the company to our excellent team, and my focus is more on product development and the long-term vision of Kabuki Strength. To do that, I need to stay away from day-to-day operations. Rudy handles all the finances, contracts, and negotiations, and I trust him 100 percent. He's a rock and a father figure to me, and the balance between his contributions and mine has been an essential element of the unprecedented success of our business.

DEVOTING MYSELF TO GRAND GOALS

It was the morning after a severe depressive episode. I woke up, shot a video, and posted it. The video was titled *Grand Goals*. In the clip, I explained that I was retiring from competitive powerlifting. I had competed at an elite level for sixteen years, set world records, and achieved almost everything I wanted to achieve in the sport. I wasn't going to stop lifting, nor retire from my public role as a strength coach and educator, but it was time to draw down the curtain on my competitive lifting career.

In its place, I would chase things that excited me, build my own platform, and express myself through lifting in ways that felt truly authentic.

Before I departed the stage, however, there were some goals I wanted to achieve. The first was to deadlift one thousand pounds. Due to my injuries, I knew that this wouldn't be possible within the rules of a competitive environment. Outside those restrictions, however, I felt that it might be. I no longer needed the validation and satisfaction that comes with winning a competition. I needed to do this for myself.

My retirement from competitive lifting came for the same reason as my divorce, my separation from significant people in my life, and the shift in my career. I knew that I could accomplish more by stepping out of an environment which had begun to feel misaligned with my vision.

Defining these boundaries and choosing mindfully where I invested my time, energy, and strength was foundational to this transition. Together with the leadership team at Kabuki Strength, I began to set up fundraisers to support charities I believed in. For example, I set up an event to raise money for a charity serving homeless people in the Portland area, particularly single mothers. The same charity also invests in a boys' house, supporting boys who have struggled with homelessness, sexual abuse, and other related issues. I was able to combine the delivery of financial aid with some speaking and motivational work for a large group of the boys living in this house. Using my strength to support people struggling with poverty became a cornerstone of my practice and continues to mean a great deal to me.

I succeeded in deadlifting 1,001 pounds, a Guinness World Record. I'm the lightest person ever to deadlift in excess of one thousand pounds. Only five other people have ever achieved the feat, all of whom weigh at least 140 pounds more than me. There are two different styles of deadlifting: conventional and sumo. I'm the only person ever to deadlift over a thousand pounds using the sumo style. I'm also the only person ever to complete repetitions with a bar weighing one thousand pounds. I completed close to three repetitions. As of 2019, all of these records remain unbroken.

When I realized that I could perform unique feats of strength to raise money for valuable causes, I broadened the scope of the charities I supported. For example, I lent my skills to the Oregon chapter of a charity named Special Olympics. To promote their cause, I undertook a thirty-day campaign in which I squatted eight hundred pounds every day for thirty days. No one had even lifted such a heavy weight so frequently, so this challenge was picked up by local media and garnered a sizeable following worldwide.

When individuals with special needs become involved in powerlifting, they often experience profound satisfaction. As their strength increases and the size of the weight that they can move increases, they see a tangible shift in what they can do. No one needs to congratulate them; they know that they've done something good and that they're improving. This self-awareness has a huge impact on their self-confidence. In addition, completing such unusual and difficult exploits provides a demonstration of what Kabuki Strength stands for. We coach people to develop robust strength, to recover quickly, and to sustain performance levels that others might dismiss as impossible. When I undertake a fundraiser, it's not only about delivering money to those who need it. It's also about teaching people that they can go beyond their perceived limitations.

During my thirty-day squat challenge, I filmed videos each day detailing my preparation and rehab. I also appeared as a guest on various podcasts, talking about what I was doing and using myself as an example. I don't like to tell people what they can do unless I can demonstrate the value of it for them. It's much more powerful to say, "This is how I did this thing that no one thought was possible," than it is simply to offer advice.

I haven't completed every challenge I've taken on, but I've always documented them so that people can see the process and, hopefully, become inspired. For example, I set myself the goal of deadlifting 880 pounds—almost a world record weight—every day for thirty days. There are only a handful of people in the world who can deadlift 880 pounds, and most of them can only do it a few times per year. I managed to do it seventeen days in a row.

This particular challenge was a fundraiser for Alex's Lemonade Stand. Alex was a little girl who was diagnosed with cancer when she was four years old. She decided to raise a million dollars for cancer research and, by the time she passed away at age eight, she had succeeded in doing exactly that. Since her passing, her charity has continued to flourish. My team and I spoke to Alex's mother for almost an hour, hearing stories about her daughter's incredible drive and the battles she fought with her cancer. It was an incredibly moving and powerful experience, and it was a privilege to support Alex's ongoing work.

I'll always be thankful for engaging in competitive powerlifting. It played a vital part in my life for many years. It was important to test myself against the best lifters in the world. Eventually, however, I was ready to walk away from that arena and put my skills to different use. I wanted to educate people, inspire people, and help those in need. Only by stripping away my identity as a competitive lifter was I able to discover a deeper and more meaningful purpose underneath.

Standing next to my Guinness World Record certificate and the image of the lift that brought me the record.

THE GENESIS OF KABUKI STRENGTH

Kabuki Strength is a practical manifestation of a shared vision—a world made better through strength. We stand on four pillars: **education**, **equipment**, **coaching**, and **charity**.

Education refers to our foundational understanding of biomechanics and movement under load, developed over many years of work with top clinicians, researchers, and athletes. Thanks to several incredible mentors, I've had the opportunity to study pain management, rehabilitation, developmental kinesiology, and several other disciplines across multiple schools of thought. As a strength athlete and coach, I have worked to adapt and deploy this new knowledge, combined with my own observations, into a pragmatic system with broad application to both athletic and nonathletic populations. These years of continuing education and practice have resulted in an integrated movement philosophy now taught around the world.

The **equipment** we design, engineer, and manufacture is a practical expression of Kabuki Strength's education goals. In a hyper-commoditized world, we choose to push boundaries and invest in the development of original tools that solve new and existing problems in novel ways. Our primary driver for new product development isn't the market, it's our understanding of how the human body should move and function in the pursuit of strength, health, and performance.

As **coaches**, we engage in productive mentorship with highly driven athletes, both locally at our facility and digitally across the world. The purposeful and disciplined execution of our educational curriculum is best seen in the fruitful coach-athlete relationships we nurture.

Charity is an expression of our deep desire to see the world and its people made better through strength. We choose to use our platform as a company to help others, to partner with valuable organizations in our community, and to bring awareness to incredible causes around the country. Considering my own story, this pillar is near and dear to my heart. I am proud to work with a team that shares the same passion for doing good in the world.

Kabuki Strength started with a single product, the ShouldeRök. It is a modern take on a classic strength training tool that has been used by Indian wrestlers for centuries, the gada. I believe the gada is the oldest-known weighted implement for the purposes of building strength and endurance. The tool, which looks like a mace, is designed to be swung overhead in a pendulum motion. This movement has a positive effect on the overall health, strength, and longevity of the entire shoulder girdle, while simultaneously reinforcing proper torso rigidity. The Rök, as it's often called, comes with in-depth educational materials on its proper application. Until I released a modern version of the gada and started the resurgence of mace swinging, very few people were familiar with it. Today, it's a common training tool, with many companies jumping on the bandwagon and providing their own versions of the product.

Since that first success, I have designed several other products in a similar vein, each one intended to improve quality of movement and decrease injury risk in athletes. At first, I didn't have the resources to create strong branding and develop powerful marketing campaigns, but the products soon began to coalesce into a brand of their own accord. Within three months of launching the company, our products were in use by Major League Baseball teams. Within two years, Kabuki Strength products were distributed extensively throughout Major League Baseball, the NFL, and collegiate sports.

In tandem with product manufacturing, I began to build an educational website to house the hours of content produced by me and my team. Today, the Kabuki Strength team regularly trains and consults collegiate and professional sports teams, along with speaking at prestigious industry events such as rehab and injury prevention symposiums. When we set up a booth at collegiate or professional shows, it is bombarded by coaches who follow our work and want to ask us questions.

Our philosophy is to provide as much education as we can for free, through YouTube and social media. This approach has paid enormous dividends and allows us to reach the consumer from a position of trust and authority. We don't believe in making things solely to boost our bottom line. Instead, we have confidence in the quality of our products and stand by everything we do. Working with professional athletes, coaches, and therapists, is a lot of fun, and the feedback we receive from both clinicians and consumers encourages and inspires us to keep pushing.

When I receive a message from someone whose life has

been positively impacted by Kabuki Strength, it makes my day. I recently received an email from someone who told me he had been struggling with back pain and had been unable to train for six months. After spending time digging into and studying our content, he made several critical changes to his breathing and posture and the pain was gone. He walked into the gym, trained pain-free, and quickly tripled his previous personal best in the squat.

Online, the ShouldeRök has received hundreds of glowingly positive reviews, in addition to the many, many testimonials I hear in person. I've heard from people who were expecting to have surgery or believed that they would never be able to lift without pain again, and who are now capable of lifting pain-free, without surgery. Not only are they moving and training again, their success feeds into other areas of their life, enabling them to passionately pursue their goals. This is much more than just lifting weights. We are in the business of changing lives. Playing a part in these transformations is incredibly rewarding and lights a fire in me both to do more and to be more.

I know from personal experience how profound such transformations can be. A few years back, I was struggling to deadlift 700 pounds. I was hitting 695 pounds, but I felt as though I had reached a ceiling. A few weeks before a big meet, I tweaked my back. It was bad. The only way

I could get out of bed was to roll. You might think that this injury would have caused me to abandon my goal of deadlifting 700 pounds at the upcoming meet. Instead, it sharpened my determination.

In the warm-up room, my strength was way down. I put 585 pounds on the bar, a weight I normally lifted with ease, and couldn't shift it. My back hurt too much. Even this setback didn't deter me. When I walked out to compete, I started at 620 pounds. What *did* change was my mindset. I realized that, with my back injured, the only way I could raise so much weight was by perfecting my positioning and timing. I set myself with enormous care and patience, making minute adjustments to my stance. I sensed that, if I was even an inch out of alignment, my back would flare up in agony when I attempted to move the bar.

Finally, my back was locked in and the only way I could move the weight was through my hips. I settled into the lift and exerted pressure. It was easy. For my second lift, I moved the weight up to 740 pounds. That, too, went up with ease. I had one more attempt and I decided to see how far I could take it. An hour earlier, I had never deadlifted more than 700 pounds. For my final attempt, I put 801 pounds on the bar.

I was nervous as hell, with my stomach twisting into a knot. I walked up to the bar, dialed in my position, and waited until I felt the moment was right. The bar moved. All 801 pounds came off the floor. That was when I knew I could do it. I finished the deadlift. I still remember that as the day I truly learned to deadlift, and tell the story as an illustration of how proper movement allows us to tap into reserves of strength we have never known we possess. It's a principle that has become the backbone of everything we do at Kabuki Strength.

HOW KABUKI STRENGTH ALMOST NEVER HAPPENED

Despite the early success of the ShouldeRök, I experienced a lot of self-doubt in the early days of Kabuki Strength. I felt that launching a company with only one product was a big risk. What if it stalled out and died? I was certain that I didn't want to return to the corporate world, and that I wanted to help people find a way through pain, so I gave serious consideration to working in health care.

I sat down for drinks with a successful doctor who was also a friend of mine, Dr. Snell. He was known around the country for his work in the field of back rehabilitation, and he was very involved in the education of other clinicians, through hosting seminars, connecting people, and acting as a mentor. As we talked, I told him that I wanted to dedicate myself to helping people get out of pain, and that I was contemplating going back to school to study physical therapy or chiropractic medicine.

He responded by asking me to clearly define my goals and, after some digging, it became clear that I wanted to have a broad, deep impact on people's lives by integrating the clinical and strength training worlds. With my passion for biomechanics and kinesiology, combined with a background as an elite lifter and strength coach, I felt that I was in a unique position to bring about tremendous change.

My friend listened to me and told me that, if that was my objective, I was never going to accomplish it by going back to school. He asked me what I would get from training as a chiropractor or a physical therapist, and I said, "credibility." "Ah," he responded. "You want to go back to school so you can get some letters after your name." It was the first time I'd thought about it in those terms, but he was correct. Much as I love working with people on an individual basis, I didn't *want* to restrict myself to working with one person at a time, as I would need to do as a physical therapist or chiropractor. I felt that I had the potential to reach far more people and have a far greater impact.

My friend continued, telling me that I would be deeply frustrated if I went back to school. He explained that I would already know 98 percent of what I'd learn in a clinical setting, and the extra 2 percent wouldn't make a major difference in my ability to deliver value. In addition, he said, the graduate programs would take four years to complete, and, with my network, I'd stay up to date with the evolving state of knowledge in the field more quickly *outside* of the classroom than inside. Instead, he suggested, it would make more sense to invest an eighth of the time and an eighth of the money into self-directed learning. He was right.

Listening to him, something clicked into place. The more I thought about it, the more I realized that I already had personal or professional relationships with many of the researchers who had played key roles in writing the books I would have studied from if I went back to school. I realized that I had been holding onto the belief that the vast body of knowledge and practical experience I had collected over the years was less valid than the attainment of another degree. I told my friend that I would continue with Kabuki Strength and, when I was standing in front of a room full of doctors, I would know that I had gained the credibility I felt was lacking.

About nine months later, Dr. Stu McGill, the world's leading researcher on back injury and spine biomechanics, invited me to deliver a presentation at a course he was teaching to over one hundred and fifty clinicians. Today, I am frequently invited to speak on a multitude of topics by some of the most respected researchers and organizations in the industry.

LESSON: A LIVING LEGACY

The life I live today is a little surreal. I have found my purpose, which I live and breathe each and every day. I spend every waking moment striving to build my legacy. It's a phenomenal feeling to know confidently that my actions have a positive impact on the world. People know that I'm here and they know that I'm making a difference. Through Kabuki Strength, I have brought original tools to market and helped thousands of people to leave pain behind. Meanwhile, through my own feats of strength, I'm walking the walk and pushing the boundaries of what's humanly possible. Most importantly, my children are growing up to understand that they can shape the world around them and create the life they wish to live. They can pursue grand goals with no fear and fully believe in their own capacity to effect change. Why? Because they see me doing the same thing, day in and day out.

In the conclusion of this book, I want to talk to you about what it means to create your own legacy. For now, though, I have a simple question for you. If a poor boy who grew up in the mountains skinning rattlesnakes can do what I've done, is there any reason that you can't? I've walked through a life that most people would find hard to imagine, let alone survive. Yet here I am, sharing my story with you, hoping that it will inspire you to fan the flames of your potential, and to choose greatness. What's stopping you?

FINDING FREEDOM IN A RULES-BASED SOCIETY

I've never liked rules and authority. Now that you know my background, you can probably understand where that tendency comes from. Beneath all the craziness and nomadic lifestyles, I believe that my parents were perpetually searching for freedom from a world that felt like four constricting walls, slowly closing in on them. They didn't want to be bound by the rules of society; rules in which they never had a say. They wanted to live the way they chose, chasing their dreams and creating their own meaning.

As I reflect on my mom's life today, I realize that she's found her version of that dream. She lives out in the boonies by herself, working rocks and making jewelry. Meanwhile, I've found a way of creating a life that feels absolutely my own *within* society. I work in a very unconventional way. I come and go from my company as I please. If I'm feeling creative, I may explore a new product or film new content. If I get tired, I take a nap. Every member of my staff understands that, if they find me asleep on the couch in the middle of the day, it's because I'm doing what I need to do for the sake of my mental and physical health. Over the years, I've often struggled to find a balance between work and rest. Now, I make my own rules and discover my own balance.

Kabuki Strength's employees are some of the most

brilliant people in the industry. As a purpose-driven organization with a clear brand identity, we don't struggle to recruit. Quite the opposite. The right people come to us because they're attracted by our purpose and want to be part of what we're doing. This is exactly the circumstance in which I met my amazing wife Jaqueline. Choose to create an environment of greatness and you will draw people toward you like a gravitational force.

With such outstanding talent at my disposal, I have no need to micromanage Kabuki Strength's employees. This gives me the freedom to hand over an enormous amount of control to people who have my complete trust. In essence, I function as a consultant within my own company. There's no specific area for which I'm responsible. Instead, I contribute to each different area as needed. I'm at the end of a highly productive, world-class company, yet I have the freedom to express myself as I need to. I'm surrounded by rules and authority, yet I feel no need to comply.

Now that you know my story, take some time to reflect on your own life. The deepest questions in life are often the simplest, but they only serve their purpose when we're truly honest with ourselves. The greatest lies you will ever tell are not to other people. They are to yourself. Find solitude, peel back the layers, and ask yourself these questions as if your life depended on it. Because it does.

Where are you going?

What do you want?

What's your vision?

What obstacles stand in your way?

I can't tell you what to value. I do believe, however, that the words in this book can inspire and equip you to take action in your own life.

As this book draws to a conclusion, I'll share with you some final thoughts on how you can use the experiences and lessons I've shared in this book to reinvent yourself.

CONCLUSION

Many of the stories I've shared in this book are incredibly personal. Even today, after writing, reading, reviewing, and rewriting these words, I still get emotional reading them. It's a little nerve wracking to put them into the public domain. I've done it because I believe in the power of story and the impact it can have on an open, receptive heart.

When I look back on the arc of my life, I'm in awe of what I've survived, and how much I've learned along the way. By sharing my life story, I hope I can convince you to believe that you, too, are far, far stronger than you think you are. In the modern world, many of us settle for an easy, comfortable life. We can avoid challenges, so we do. My hope is that this memoir will provide you with the momentum you need to start bringing about change, to start asking yourself the hard and simple questions, and to start building a legacy. Discover a mission that feels deeply personal to you. Conquer the fear that holds you back. Be an agent of change, not comfort.

When your guts begin to twist and you feel like you're standing on the edge of a cliff, recognize that this is nothing more than confirmation that you're walking on hallowed ground that leads to your true self. Don't hide from that sign. Follow it and fight for it. It will take you where you need to go.

I've had a very unusual life. While I wouldn't change a thing about my experiences, let's be clear that you don't need to emulate the craziness of my life to do great things. If there's one lesson that I want you to take from my story, it's that you can *choose* what matters to you and pursue it with passion, despite your circumstances. The reason I've told you where I come from is that I want you to understand and *believe* how far it's possible to move the needle. If I can go from being a poor boy, sleeping in a wilderness shack through the depths of winter, to one of the strongest men in the world, helping thousands of people, what can you do?

MANY TYPES OF STRENGTH

I'm known globally as a creator and purveyor of strength

education and products. This book, however, fills a gap. It enables me to talk about the other, equally important aspects of strength that aren't covered by the work I do with Kabuki Strength. These are the mental, emotional, and even spiritual elements that make strength a universal virtue, worthy of pursuit by all.

Strength is your capacity to bend your will to living the life you choose. Marie Curie wisely said: "Life is not easy for any of us. But what of that? We must have perseverance and above all confidence in ourselves. We must believe that we are gifted for something and that this thing must be attained." Life gives each of us our fair share of opportunities to experience challenge and hardship, whether we ask for them or not. These are valuable, important moments that we can use to grow stronger, to adapt, and to persevere. Sometimes strength can be the difference between life and death.

Perseverance is action derived from a pure belief in your own strength, even in what seems like total defeat. Just like Pat and my father, I struggled with alcohol. I've stepped close to the edge, lured by the deceitful whispers of the devil who promises that ending it all will bring comfort. My redemption has been a powerful self-realization that my identity is not found in my circumstances or in what *happens* to me. I am strong. I am my own will made manifest in the world.

As you grow in self-awareness, your understanding of your strengths becomes more precise. Be intentional. Take the time to explore your passions and figure out which strengths you most want to cultivate. I don't want you to settle for the role of consumer in this world. I urge you to master the necessary skills to contribute in a meaningful fashion, and to use those skills to make a difference in your own life and the lives of others. It's far too easy to fall into the trap of working a job you hate and living for the weekend. Find a way of breaking out of that paradigm. Don't be afraid of trying hard. Don't be afraid of failing or looking like an idiot. There are no prizes for being cool and collected, but achieving nothing of value. Leave your mark on the world.

Grow your strengths through purposeful and diligent practice. Your personal evolution is rooted in perpetual action and reaction—the antithesis of complacency. You never know when something will click into place and you'll fall in love with a discipline that can change your life. On a whim, I decided to compete in a strength competition, thinking it would be an interesting one-off experience. Instead, I enjoyed years of competitive powerlifting, held numerous world records, and now harness my love of the iron to perform feats of strength and support causes I believe in. I could have held back, worried because I wasn't sure how to perform a deadlift. If I'd done that, I might never have taken part in a sport that has become a cornerstone of my life.

You don't need to be good at something before you try it, but you must be resolute in your efforts when you choose to master something. Mediocrity is the ugly, fatal disease of wasted potential and eternal regret. In the words of Dante Aligheri:

And I—my head oppressed by horror—said: "Master, what is it that I hear? Who are those people so defeated by their pain?" And he to me: "This miserable way is taken by the sorry souls of those who lived without disgrace and without praise. They now commingle with the coward angels, the company of those who were not rebels nor faithful to their God, but stood apart. The heavens, that their beauty not be lessened, have cast them out, nor will deep Hell receive them. Even the wicked cannot glory in them."

In practice and in heart, I regularly repeat these four words: "There is always more." Perfection is not our destination. Instead, we follow the never-ending trail of joy and tears, knowing full well that it has no end. The alternative is unacceptable.

As you persevere and find success, the sweet voice of praise from your own mind and those around you will whisper, "You are amazing. You did it." Acknowledge that voice, but don't allow it to seduce you. Instead of dwelling on my successes, I see clearly the areas where I'm still growing and improving. However good you think you are, you can always be better. This is the nature of ceaseless self-improvement—you can always dig a little deeper, work a little harder, and push a little further than before. There is always more.

PRIORITIZATION IN REVERSE

My approach to prioritization is different from most. I don't start with a list of all the things I need to accomplish, then try to pack as many of them as I can into my day. Instead, I start by determining what's *not* essential. What fluff can I cut out of my life? What pointless tasks can I say "no" to today? If you try to make everything a priority, your only success will be in making a really nice list. When the nonessential is stripped away, that which is truly crucial to your life emerges. Be critical and honest about how you spend your time, because it's yours to lose.

Your relationships—the people you choose to invest in and be vulnerable with—are among the most valuable and important components of your value system. Choose them wisely. There is little virtue in being a people pleaser, and the quality of your relationships matters far more than the quantity. Don't be afraid to cut those connections that aren't aligned with your vision, supporting you, or challenging you to become better. Sour relationships bring a great emotional burden. When they are gone, you will be armed with a newfound freedom and energy to invest in those you choose. The key is to separate real needs from what is merely convenient, or worse, counterproductive. There are only twenty-four short hours in a day: are you using your time and mental resources wisely?

I am convinced that many people spend 80 percent of their time doing meaningless things that add little real value to their lives. Blissfully unaware, life lives them. Discipline starts when you stop wasting your life doing stupid things. Make an honest, detailed inventory of your days over the course of a week. Is how you spend your time reflective of your values and your vision? Cut out the waste, and you'll be amazed at how much time you have to act on your vision. It's not easy and it takes a lot of discipline. I don't get to follow every whim or do everything I want to. The pay-off, however, is that I go to sleep every night with full confidence that I am fully *alive* and doing the work required to go where I want to go. Don't half-ass everything, whole-ass what really matters.

Find your vision and use it as a north star, faithfully guiding your actions and helping you to discern what you most need to engage in. Bringing a vision to fruition takes time in the trenches, doing hard, unpleasant work that will wear you down. Despair and defeat will lurk silently in the corners, waiting to pounce. There will be times when you feel as though you're working harder than everyone around you and still not moving forward. Through thick and thin, always keep in mind that action aligned with vision will bear fruit.

As we discussed in chapter four, there is a stark distinction between a dream and a vision. Everyone dreams. Some of us even live in dreams. To have vision is to know who you are, what you value, and what you need to do. It is an understanding of the work that is to come and a willingness to undertake that work.

WHAT TO DO NEXT

As this book draws to a close, I have some homework for you. On the following pages, you will find a worksheet consisting of six foundational questions I want you to ask yourself. Find some moments of solitude, peer deep into your heart, and put ink on paper in the space provided. One of the great gifts of self-reflection is that it comes with an inbuilt lie detector. You will know if you are lying to yourself.

There's no hiding place in life. If you fabricate your answers, you will only cheat yourself. Be honest.

What excites you in life?

What value can you add to the world? What contribution can you make?

What do you want to learn?

What type of people do you want around you?

How do you want to spend your time?

What challenges do you need to overcome?

It's a bit harder to be dishonest with yourself in writing, isn't it? Keep this book and the answers you have written nearby; reading them will serve you well during inevitable moments of weakness and discouragement. If you are comfortable sharing your answers with me, and me alone, please email them to chris@theeagleandthedragon.com. You can also download additional worksheets from my website.

A FINAL REQUEST

My intent is for this book to leave you different than it found you. There is power in story, and my hope is that these words will inspire you and radically alter your perceptions about what's possible in your life. If you've found value in these pages, I have one small request of you. Please share this book with others.

The best way to do that is with a personal recommendation. Lend your copy of the book to someone you think will benefit from it or buy it as a gift for a friend's birthday. If there is someone that immediately comes to mind as a person who *needs* to read this book, buy them a copy. If your hunch is right, your gift may mean more to them than you'll ever know.

Feel free to reach out to me on social media, too. I'm on Instagram, at @mad_scientist_duffin, and also on

LinkedIn. You can also contact me via my company website, kabukistrength.com, or my personal website, christopherduffin.com, where you can also subscribe to my newsletter.

In my guise as the Mad Scientist of Strength, I cohost the Strength Chat podcast with the Wizard of Training and the esteemed Doctor Rudolph. You can find us on all the popular podcast platforms.

Here's to your strength.

ACKNOWLEDGMENTS

While I lacked mentors or role models in my earlier years and was mostly left to figure out the world on my own, it would be remiss of me not to acknowledge the influence my parents had on my life. Like the rest of us, they were a long way from perfect. Nonetheless, I'm forever grateful for the positive qualities they instilled in me during those formative years. My mother gave me strength, a powerful work ethic, perseverance, and an indomitable will to forge my own path in the world. My father taught me to be passionate about life and to wholeheartedly pursue the things that bring me meaning and joy. My stepfather taught me the spirit of living in the moment and enjoying life as it comes. Collectively, they instilled in me the importance of intellectual, physical, and creative pursuits.

My first mentor was my wrestling coach, Rusty Zysset,

who saw past my rough outward appearance and invested in me. He encouraged me, supported me, and taught me that there is no shortcut to success in life. He made sure I understood that the discipline we practice molds and shapes us, even when no one else is looking.

Rudy Kadlub is my business partner, with whom I co-founded Kabuki Strength. More than that, he is my close friend and mentor. Rudy has taught me much about business, life, and family—wisdom I strive constantly to emulate. I can't imagine working to build a legacy with anyone else, and I trust him with my life. He is a father figure for me as an adult, and I cherish our relationship.

Huge gratitude goes out to a number of mentors who gave me a shot as I transitioned from the manufacturing industry to the world of biomechanics, strength, and performance. These individuals taught me much, supported me, and opened doors for me to grow even before I was known in the public sphere. Dr. Phillip Snell tops the list, along with Dr. Stuart McGill, Dr. Craig Liebenson, and Dr. Kelly Starrett. I'm honored that these brilliant and influential professionals now serve on the advisory board of Kabuki Strength.

Dave Tate of EliteFTS has been a constant source of guidance as I transitioned into the strength industry and worked to build Kabuki Strength. Mark Bell was the first person to push me in this direction and has actively encouraged me for more than a decade. I'm thankful to both of these noble and successful men for inspiring and supporting me.

Without the help of the team at Scribe Media, Rob Wolf Petersen, and Andrei Miclea, I wouldn't have been able to complete this book in a manner that does the story and message justice.

Last, but by no means least, I want to thank the incredible people who make up our team at Kabuki Strength. We've never really hired people the traditional way using job postings or recruiters. Instead, we've discovered that if we express our mission, values, and vision in all of our actions, the right people will find us. Rudy and I have enjoyed long careers as leaders, and without hesitation we agree that Kabuki Strength's employees are unparalleled when it comes to commitment, skill, and passion. It is an incredible feeling to work with a group of people who share a common goal, and who eagerly invest their time and energy into our vision of making the world a better place through strength. I can't thank each of them enough for their inexhaustible dedication and diligence.

ABOUT THE AUTHOR

CHRIS DUFFIN is the co-founder and chief engineer at Kabuki Strength, an organization devoted to optimizing human performance and making the world a better place through strength. He previously worked as a corporate executive and has turned around automotive, aerospace, heavy equipment, and high-tech manufacturing industries.

Chris was previously ranked number one in the world in various powerlifting disciplines and has held numerous world records. Now retired, he is known for his industry-changing innovations and education in the strength and clinical worlds. He's a leading speaker on topics related to strength and human movement, and performs insane feats of strength to help charities and organizations whose work he believes in.